T0328511

Listening to Colonial History

Anette Hoffmann

LISTENING TO COLONIAL HISTORY

Echoes of Coercive Knowledge Production
in Historical Sound Recordings
from Southern Africa

Basler Afrika Bibliographien

©2023 The authors
©2023 The photographers
©2023 Basler Afrika Bibliographien

Basler Afrika Bibliographien
Namibia Resource Centre & Southern Africa Library
Klosterberg 23
PO Box
4001 Basel
Switzerland
www.baslerafrika.ch

CARL SCHLETTWEIN
STIFTUNG

The Basler Afrika Bibliographien is part of the Carl Schlettwein Foundation

Translated and revised by Anette Hoffmann on the basis of her book *Kolonialgeschichte hören. Das Echo gewaltsamer Wissensproduktion in historischen Tondokumenten aus dem südlichen Afrika,* first published by Mandelbaum Verlag in Vienna, 2020.
English language editing by Rosemary Lombard.
Cover designed by Candice Turvey.

ISBN 978-3-906927-39-8

CONTENTS

Fig. 1: Unnamed man, probably a teacher from
Berseba, listening to a sound recording. Detail from a
photograph by Hans Lichtenecker, German Southwest Africa (Namibia), 1931.

PREFACE

Echoes are heard with a delay. They arrive as distorted, perhaps abbreviated, often attenuated resonances of something said, shouted, or sung elsewhere. As travelling reverberations, echoes may resound with the occasion of speaking or singing, not informing listeners where they come from, or who is speaking. As echo, the voice is transformed; sometimes it multiplies and becomes polyphonic. Bouncing and delayed, echoes carry gaps of meaning, and thus become disorienting to listeners. Their source, but also their intended audience, might remain obscure. To the archival echo of colonial history we have begun to listen only recently.

In Ovid's *Metamorphoses*, the nymph Echo *(vocalis nymphe)* is punished by the goddess Juno for distracting her with beguiling talk. The sanction or measure against distracting talk for Echo is her disablement: the loss of her ability to speak. From then on, she can only repeat abbreviated, and therefore distorted, versions of someone else's words. This durable detachment of voice from person has major implications: the figure of Echo becomes a repercussing automaton, the host of a mimicking voice that is severed from (her) intentions. Sounding like the acoustic materialization of *palilalia*[1] places each of Echo's utterances outside of meaningful articulation or communication and thus is the verdict of her social death.[2] When she falls in love with Narcissus, she cannot respond, let alone address him, but must merely repeat his words, and, as Joan W. Scott tells us, her response as Echo can only be a deformed fragment of Narcissus' words.[3] Her inability to speak or respond as a person, that is, to speak according to her own intentions and in her own(ed) voice, leads to Narcissus' rejection of Echo. In grief her body withers away until nothing remains of her but a voice *(vox manet)*. Thus her voice becomes the disembodied, dislocated sound effect we know as echo.

---

1   The compulsive repetition of syllables and words, described as a tic or pathological disorder of speech.

2   For Petra Gehrmann, Echo's voice as *Wiederholungstimme* (voice as repetition) is therefore lifeless, yet unable to die – see "Die Wiederholungsstimme: Über die Strafe der Echo", Doris Kolesch and Sybille Krämer (eds.), *Stimme*, Frankfurt am Main: Suhrkamp, 2006.

3   Joan W. Scott, "Fantasy Echo: History and the Construction of Identity", *Critical Inquiry* 27 (2) 2001, p. 201.

Gayatri Chakravorty Spivak's take on Echo suggests reconsidering the tale – arguably in response to the discussion of her famous, perhaps notorious, article "Can the subaltern speak?" – by offering a reading that seeks to fathom the elusive trace of female subalternity in hegemonic discourse and the colonial archive. In her reading, the myth of Narcissus (as told by Ovid) is the tale of self as an object of knowledge, whereas the figure of Echo is staged as a respondent *as such*, albeit responding with a twist – creating gaps of meaning and intelligibility, and leaving us with an ambiguous trace. While Ovid's tale narrates the instance of a *complete* severance of agency or intention from speech in the instance of Echo's reverberations (that become a mere parroting, and thus are no longer "human"), Spivak grapples with the possibility of an ambiguity withheld in his tale. She writes:

> Throughout the reported exchange between Narcissus and Echo she behaves according to her punishment and gives back the end of each statement. Ovid "quotes" her, except when Narcissus asks: *Quid... me fugis?* (Why do you fly from me?). Caught in the discrepancy between second person interrogative (*fugis*) and the imperative (*fugi*), Ovid cannot allow her to *be*, even Echo, so that Narcissus, flying from her, could have made of the ethical structure of response a fulfilled antiphon.[4]

In other words, when Narcissus asks "why do you fly from me?" according to Spivak, Echo's response (which is withheld in Ovid's text) would have been "fly from me". This interpretative move considers the possibility of a reverberation that carries a shift of meaning, a difference, which cannot be appropriated by that which it repeats.[5] In this way, Spivak's reading of the myth of Echo creates a space of ambivalence in which the echo that is almost, but never quite, the same opens a space of ambiguity or alterity that allows for the possibility of a "faint residue"[6] of an uncontainable, yet perhaps uncertain, intention.

---

4   Gayatri Chakravorty Spivak, "Echo", *New Literary History*, 25 (1) *Culture and Everyday Life*, Winter 1993, p. 25, italics in the original.
5   See Jane Hiddleston, "Spivak's Echo: Theorizing Otherness and the Space of Response", *Textual Practice* 21 (4), 2007, p. 627.
6   *Ibid.*

Echo's voice is "stable-yet-unstable, same-yet-different, and non-originary".[7] Whereas the difference between Narcissus's interrogative phrase (why do you fly from me?) and her answer that involuntarily must turn into an imperative (fly from me!) marks the impossibility of echoing as sameness, and designates the asymmetric positions of Narcissus and Echo, it is Ovid's position to fill in the lacuna. Which, as Spivak tells us, is impossible: the account of what happened is never quite what happened – but always a belated interpretation, which can only fill the gap with a difference. Echo, writes Spivak, guards this dissimilarity, since her imitating-yet-not-quite-the-same response must always slightly alter the meaning of the phrase, which is her "punishment turned into reward, a deconstructive lever for future users."[8]

The notion of echo offers a starting point from which to conceptualize particular voice recordings as sonic traces from the colonial archive as neither merely signifying the theoretically "untouchable" figure of the subaltern[9] – nor marking an unproblematic recuperation of subjective agency in collections of sound recordings. In this book I engage with historical voice recordings as alternative historical sources, reverberating with several instances of narrative agency, which, for instance, surface in the choice of the topics and tropes that appear to be out of sync with their archival position as examples of language. These utterances are never entirely contained as examples of language, and leave open a space of resonance.

In Gayatri Spivak's decolonial interpretation of the speaking position inhabited by the nymph Echo in Ovid's *Metamorphoses*, Echo appears as perpetually responding; she cannot speak without prompting. Her take on subaltern speaking positions resonates strongly with my understanding

7   Spivak: Echo, p. 27.
8   *Ibid.*
9   Hiddleston, p. 624, writes: "Furthermore, with perhaps more nuance Peter Hallward criticizes Spivak's concept of the subaltern for positing her voice as singular and inaccessible, and for failing to think through the means by which she might consolidate her identity and voice. For Hallward, 'the subaltern, in other words, is the theoretically untouchable, the altogether-beyond-relation: the attempt to "relate" to the subaltern defines what Spivak quite appropriately names an "impossible ethical singularity". The result is apparently that the critic deprives the subaltern of a voice while endlessly theorizing and retheorizing the mechanics of her own critical, and unavoidably Western, enunciation.'" See Peter Hallward, *Absolutely Postcolonial: Writing Between the Singular and the Specific*, 2001, p. 30.

of historical speech recordings, in which the speech acts that were record-ed were determined by questions, which we, as listeners in the presence, cannot hear. Echo's responses are abbreviated or distorted repetitions of these questions or of what has been said. Because her voice is dissociated from her will, what she articulates appears detached from her intentions. Echo, forever responding, nevertheless creates additional meaning, which can be found in the displacement or distortion, or is carried by her enig-matic responses to questions we cannot hear. Her voice remains. Outliving her speaking body, it lives on as an acoustic enigma. Via Spivak, I suggest listening to the echoes that resound from the colonial archive as the faint, often fragmented, acoustic resonances of subaltern speaking positions. Listening to the colonial archive, we, as listeners in the present, can hear historical sound recordings as the sonic remains of situations of knowl-edge production, as acoustic traces of speakers, and as starting points for hearing aspects of colonial history.[10] The recordings this book engages with are not "voices from the past"; rather, they have reached the present as their mediatized echoes. Listening to them, we hear the answers to ques-tions that remain occluded, but also responses to researchers' attitudes and requests, as well as statements of speakers that have, fortunately, survived in the acoustic recordings.

We can listen to these acoustic recording from the colonial archive as abbreviated, mediated, and often distorted traces of speech acts, songs and stories, which imply the modification of the voices that spoke, but also contain reverberations of accounts, messages, interventions, com-mentary and critique, at times articulated from subaltern positions, in the process of producing an archive of languages. Echo may be good to think with because it allows for the re-surfacing of responses that reside in the interstices of formalized speech acts, appear as parts of grammatical examples, or at times surface as direct commentary in the recordings.

This book grew out of the idea of listening to what is left of histor-ical sound recordings in the archive. It is an attempt to approach colonial history as a listener and to interrogate unwritten acoustic sources, in order to be able to include other speakers and speaking positions, from within the colonial archive.

10   For echo as history see Carolyn Birdsall, *Nazi Soundscapes: Sound, Technology and Urban Space in Germany, 1933–1945*, Amsterdam: University of Amsterdam Press, 2012.

Most of the chapters of this book focus on one specific collection of acoustic recordings. This collection of audio recordings, most of which were produced with Naro speakers in the Kalahari in 1908 by the Austrian anthropologist Rudolf Pöch, was released as a CD in 2003, along with a booklet.[11] The CD contains acoustic recordings and their documentation in all archival states: recordings which were re-translatable, as well as those which defied such attempts due to their sound quality, recordings which came with little or no information on the speakers, or which were documented incorrectly, and those which were documented according to the archival requirements of the *Phonogrammarchiv* in Vienna. Several of the recordings came with transcriptions, of which some were more plausible than others, and some came with no transcriptions at all. Many recordings were only summarized, and these written summaries often did not correspond with their acoustic content. Some of the people recorded could be identified visually in the photographic collection; others do not appear in the visual record. The researcher's notebooks of the days during which the recordings took place are lost. Thus, little can be learned of some speakers. The recordings contain example sentences, narratives, but also harsh comments and insults (which do not appear in the written record). The work of re-associating the recordings with the rest of the objects that the Austrian anthropologist brought to Vienna was often possible, although translating the recordings proved to be a difficult task. Naro, the language spoken on most of the recordings, is not written by all of its approximately 20000 speakers in Namibia and Botswana; it is rarely taught in schools.[12] The historical marginalization of Naro speakers continues to affect the lives of many of them in the present.

Fortunately, Job Morris, Naro speaker and San rights activist from D'kar, Botswana, agreed to engage in close listening, to (re)translate and (re)interpret the recordings and to discuss aspects of their meaning with me. The re-interpretation of the recordings would have been impossible without him. For vital support in the process of finding translators, and for listening to the recordings together, I thank Joram Useb at !Khwa ttu,

11   Schüller, Dietrich (ed.), *Rudolf Pöch's Kalahari Recordings (1908): Sound Documents from the Phonogrammarchiv of the Austrian Academy of Sciences: The Complete Historical Collections 1899–1950, Series 7*, Vienna: OAW 2003.
12   See Eureka Baneka Mokibelo, "Why We Drop Out of School: Voices of San School Drop Outs in Botswana", *Australian Journal of Indigenous Education*, 43 (2), 2014.

Jos Thorne in Cape Town, and Kileni Fernando and Apollia Dabe in Windhoek.

This research and the present publication were made possible by the generous support of the *Volkswagen Foundation*, with the grant called *Originalitätsverdacht*, which I received in 2018. Special thanks are due for the enthusiastic mentoring of the project by Nataliya Moor and Sebastian Schneider. For the invitation to attach my project to the Institute for Cultural Studies at Humboldt University in Berlin, I thank Britta Lange and Christian Kassung; for the practical implementation of this connection, I thank Nadia Shamsan and Jana Gottke. My initial reflections on this collection from the Kalahari as historical source material were facilitated by a fellowship at the Research Center for Material Culture in Leiden (2016), for which I thank Wayne Modest, Ninja Rijnks-Kleikamp, and Bart Barendregt (Institute for Cultural Anthropology and Development Sociology at Leiden University).

Research on the literature and the consultation of Dorothea Bleek's notes on her audio recordings at the University of Cape Town were made possible with the generous support of a University of Cape Town travel grant, which I received as an honorary research associate of the Archive and Public Culture Research Initiative (APC) in November 2016. My ongoing position as a fellow at APC facilitated the discussion of an early version of my work on this sound collection at the Research Workshop there that same year. For this I thank Carolyn Hamilton and my colleagues at APC who discussed a first draft of the first chapter in a workshop in 2018. As a senior researcher, I organized a series of workshops on "knowing by ear", which enabled fundamental discussion and collective listening sessions with colleagues and students at APC. For vivid debates and their intellectual engagement on these topics that still resonate with me, I thank Zuleiga Adams, June Bam, Memory Biwa, Joanne Bloch, Mbongiseni Buthelezi, David Cohen, Ana Deumert, Alexandra Dodd, Jo-Anne Duggan, Erica de Greef, Carolyn Hamilton, Duane Jethro, Bodhisattva Kar, Alirio Karina, Dishon Kweya, Rosemary Lombard, Athambile Masola, George Mahashe, Grant McNulty, Renate Meyer, Thokozani Mhlambi, Philip Miller, Litheko Modisane, Susana Molins-Lliteras, Nashilongweshipwe Mushaandja, Michael Nixon, Rehana Odendaal, Debra Pryor, Himal Ramji, Regina Sarreiter, Thuthuka Sibisi, Nick Shepherd, Katleho Shoro,

Anthony Sloan, Cara Stacey, Hedley Twidle, John Wright, Niklas Zimmer, and all others I may have omitted to name here.

For permission to work with the relevant archival objects and practical assistance in doing so, I thank the *Phonogrammarchiv* in Vienna, especially Gerda Lechleitner, Kerstin Klenke, and Clemens Gütl; the *Naturhistorisches Museum* (Natural History Museum) in Vienna, especially Margit Berner and Wolfgang Reichmann; the *Filmarchiv Austria*, especially Anna Dobrink and Nikolaus Wostry; the *Weltmuseum* (World Museum) in Vienna, especially Nadja Haumberger; the archive of the *Department für Evolutionäre Anthropologie* (Department of Evolutionary Anthropology) at the University of Vienna, especially Katarina Matiasek; and Special Collections at the University of Cape Town, especially Renate Meyer. For editing the audio recordings, I thank Axel Rab; for digitizing documents from Special Collections at UCT, I thank the Digitization Unit and Niklas Zimmer.

For indispensable conversations that accompanied my work on this book, I thank Britta Lange and Jos Thorne and the first readers of the manuscript (in German), Margit Berner, Dag Henrichsen, and Ruth Sonderegger. For the very productive collaboration during the work on the German version of this book I thank the *Mandelbaum Verlag* in Vienna, specifically Elke Smodic, Michael Baiculescu and Simon Nagy. For discussion and conversations on Rudolf Pöch's travels and forays, and practices of "collecting/looting" in southern Africa more generally, the politics regarding these collections, and sound archives, I thank Carolyn Birdsall, Jannik Franzen, Werner Hillebrecht, Sophie Schasiepen, Jonathan Sterne, Holger Stoecker, and Anne Storch. For her beautiful design of the cover I thank Candice Turvey; for careful (and patient) editing and listening to the sound files, I thank Rosemary Lombard. I am very grateful to the Carl Schlettwein Foundation and the Basler Afrika Bibliographien for publishing this book. For her patient and attentive work with this revised English version I thank Petra Kerckhoff (publishing house of the Basler Afrika Bibliographien).

1 PHONOGRAPH, ARCHIVE, SWALLOW

*This also means that the lack of understanding
is not based solely on the words. It is generally based on the
situation of the speakers themselves*

Jacques Rancière

The colonial archive[13] seems to swallow words. It has gulped down entire sentences; it has made texts disappear. Not all words that disappeared from the archive were erased in the same way. Some words were deleted immediately, others faded gradually. The disappearance of words did not always follow straightforward intentions; neither did it occur by chance.

---

13 I understand the colonial archive primarily as a discursive formation, which determined what was preserved, categorized and documented as knowledge by whom, for which purposes, and in what way. This discursive formation includes collections of documents and objects, the ordering systems according to which they were arranged, as well as the implementation of practices and institutions of preservation. The colonial archive is based on paradigms and epistemic constellations, which described, explored, categorized and sought to inventory subjugated territories, people, and resources. These include languages, musical forms, and objects. The colonial archive was shaped by, and helped to constitute, imperial powers, ideas and goals. Accordingly, it is not limited to the period of direct colonial rule and places or regions that were colonized. As an epistemic formation and as a repository for documentation of colonial knowledge production, which served projects of colonization, made them possible and was in turn informed by them, it determines what is available and what is not, what can be read, seen and heard, who speaks and who must remain silent in the present. The question of how historiographies written in the present, yet based on past collections, could escape the colonial archive's logic has been discussed for several years. Historical audio recordings that date back to colonial linguistics, comparative musicology, anthropology, and folklore, are part of this knowledge production and archive. See Ann Laura Stoler, *Along the Archival Grain: Epistemic Anxieties and Colonial Common Sense*, Princeton and London: Princeton University Press 2009; Partha Chatterjee, "After Subaltern Studies", *Economic and Political Weekly* XLVII (35), 2012; Ramón Grosfoguel, "The Epistemic Decolonial Turn", *Cultural Studies* 21 (2), 2007; Carolyn Hamilton et al. (eds.), *Refiguring the Archive*, Cape Town: David Philip 2002; Michel-Rolph Trouillot, *Silencing the Past: Power and the Production of History*, Boston: Beacon Press 1995; Premesh Lalu, *The Deaths of Hintsa: Postapartheid South Africa and the Shape of Recurring Pasts*, Cape Town: HSRC Press 2009; Gyan Prakash, "Subaltern Studies as Postcolonial Criticism", *American Historical Review* 99 (5), 1994; Gyan Prakash, "The Impossibility of Subaltern History", *Nepantla* 1 (2), 2000. See also Michel Foucault, *Archäologie des Wissens*, Frankfurt am

In particular, spoken words were made unavailable. Some of the utterances which were swallowed were not deleted irreversibly. In some cases, what was said or sung can be retrieved on acoustic files, even if performed speech or the lyrics of a song have long become fragments, phrases which are now wedged between the hissing and rumbling of wax cylinder recordings, and the historical conditions of the moments of speaking or singing cannot be reconstructed easily.

Regarding the systematic loss of words, the question is not merely which words have become unavailable, but also *whose* words were deleted from the record, were muted, or became that which the archive does not know, or want to know of itself, and which have become the muffled echo of colonial knowledge production. If collections have not burned down and archive buildings have not collapsed; if no extraneous violence has triggered the loss of documents, particularly words which were once spoken or sung by those to whom colonial knowledge production did not grant positions to speak have become obscure.

The archive has not merely swallowed utterances that were heard as unintelligible comments or unsolicited words, which were relegated to the margins of projects of colonial knowledge production. Even those words, which were recorded as specimens for the collections of linguists, musicologists or ethnographers, often disappeared from the written record, and thus fell silent in the archive. The processes of swallowing, misplacing, and muting are not necessarily concluded. Sometimes, as with recordings in Khoekhoegowab that form part of a particular audio collection from Namibia (then South West Africa) that dates back to 1931, spoken texts were excised from catalogues of items in the 21st century. In the description of this collection of recordings, the word *"Hottentot"*, which once labelled this language and its speakers in a racializing manner, has been removed because it is now considered inappropriate for publication. The language in question, Khoekhoegowab, is one of the national languages of Namibia. It is unlikely that speakers of this language have ever referred to it as *"Hottentot"*. However, instead of replacing the offensive colonial term, when this "correction" was made for the catalogue, the designation of language was simply removed. This is not a minor decision. It

Main: Suhrkamp 1981; Knut Ebeling and Stephan Günzel, *Archivologie: Theorien des Archivs in Philosophie, Medien und Künsten,* Berlin: Kadmos 2009.

accounts for serious structural slippages by demonstrating that recordings that had been organized according to racial categories and languages, and never according to content or genre, could still not be indexed according to other categories in 2006. Thus, the deletion of the derogatory name for a language has led to the *de facto* disappearance of a third of the collection of historical recordings from the printed, annotated catalogue of the wax cylinders in the Berlin *Phonogramm-Archiv*.[14]

Historically, the systematic disappearance of spoken words in the archive was preceded by recording situations, which were set up according to colonial epistemic practices, informed by racist assumptions, which operated within and/or generated asymmetrical power structures. Subsequently, particular disciplinary and institutional decisions created a durable archival order in which the speakers of the historical recordings were detached from their photographs, from life casts that were produced of their faces, and perhaps also from objects that may have belonged to them, in the process of organizing the spoils of a specific expedition or project according to disciplinary logic.[15]

The recurring scene of speaking into a phonograph, in which informants were asked to perform, yet were not understood to be addressing the situation at hand, can be described with Rancière's concept of *mésentente*. This has mostly been translated as "dissent" or "political disagreement".[16] Here I refer to *mésentente* as a fundamental disagreement at the moment of recording that served the extraction of knowledge. Words were recorded, for example, for linguistic research, and while these spoken words were clearly perceived as language and had been predefined as being of

14 Susanne Ziegler, *Die Wachszylinder des Berliner Phonogramm-Archivs*, Berlin: Veröffentlichungen des Ethnologischen Museums Berlin 2006, p. 215. *"Buschmann"* as a term which describes a language (which does not exist) had not been removed from this catalogue.

15 Aníbal Quijano, "The Coloniality of Power, Eurocentrism, and Latin America", *Nepantla* 1 (3), 2000, and "Coloniality and Modernity/Rationality", *Cultural Studies* 21 (2–3), 2007; Sebastian Garbe, "Das Projekt Modernität/Kolonialität: Zum theoretischen/ akademischen Umfeld des Konzepts der Kolonialität der Macht", Sebastian Garbe and Pablo Qintero (eds.), *Kolonialität der Macht: De/Koloniale Konflikte zwischen Theorie und Praxis*, Münster: Unrast Verlag, 2013.

16 Jacques Rancière, *Das Unvernehmen*, Frankfurt am Main: Suhrkamp 1995; Ruth Sonderegger, "What One Does (Not) Hear: Approaching Canned Voices Through Rancière", Anette Hoffmann (ed.), *What We See: Reconsidering an Anthropometrical Collection: Images, Voices and Versioning*, Basel: Basler Afrika Bibliographien, 2009.

interest for linguists, they were at the same time not heard as semantically meaningful spoken texts. Utterances would thus be recorded, yet were rarely conceived of as critical responses to, or comments on, this process of knowledge production. This recurring moment of word-deafness on the part of the researchers, their tenacious unwillingness to understand comments by those studied, was thus not simply the result of a language barrier. Instead, in many cases it was the consequence of the asymmetrical relationship between researchers and speakers.

The incongruence of the recording situation has had durable effects: spoken words of people who had already been categorized according to fantasized "racial criteria" were not heard by the person who recorded them, the semantic content of their utterances was considered inconsequential to the project of knowledge production and thus casually or deliberately omitted from the archival record. Words and sentences that were recorded, but were not heard or understood by those who recorded them, were later not available for the archival index. In other words: this iterative or regular historical moment of *mésentente* has shaped practices of acoustic archiving. Following the logic of colonial knowledge production, even the clearest words, the most urgent pleas, and the sharpest criticisms, were organized in sound archives and scientific collections as either linguistic examples of speech or specimens of music. This mostly took place in a process of linguistic documentation which purged spoken texts of their semantic meaning. In this way, statements that were spoken into the phonograph's funnel, and were actually registered acoustically, subsequently disappeared from the archival record. Thus, paradoxically, although the practice of sound recording created speech acts as stable objects on (more-or-less) durable carrying media, the words that were uttered did not, and still rarely do appear in the indexes of archives and collections. The processes of deleting or discarding spoken or sung words, or occluding the meaning of utterances, accounts, or narratives from the indexes of archives, are thus the consequence of an interplay of the selective, heritable word-deafness of colonial knowledge production – which did not hear the utterances of those who were studied as meaningful spoken texts – combined with the tenacious afterlife or, rather, the unchecked continuity of coloniality in archives and museums.[17]

17   Anette Hoffmann, "Kolonialität", Daniel Morat and Hansjakob Ziemer (eds.), *Hand-*

Since the advent of phonography in the late 19th century, an innumerable number of words have been recorded acoustically: as songs, narratives, and stories, as poems, and prayers, as staged dialogues, or example sentences, as series of numbers and as examples of intonation.[18] Recordings have been produced for the study of languages, for comparative musicology, and for the research of narrative traditions in non-Western cultures. These historical recordings that were produced by linguists, ethnologists, and musicologists were often recorded in formerly colonized countries. Yet, German researchers also exploited what they saw as opportunities to record foreign people who performed in shows and on fairgrounds of colonial metropolises for instance in Berlin. During World War I, the *Königlich Preußische Phonographische Kommission* (Royal Prussian Phonographic Commission) was founded with the aim of recording language examples in German prisoner-of-war camps. This resulted in the production of hundreds of acoustic recordings, now held by the Berlin *Lautarchiv*.[19] Once acoustically preserved, these early recordings were kept

buch Sound: Geschichte - Begriffe - Ansätze, Stuttgart: Metzler, 2018; Ann Laura Stoler, *Duress: Imperial Durabilities in Our Times,* Durham and London: Duke University Press, 2016.

18 Erika Brady, *A Spiral Way: How the Phonograph Changed Ethnography,* Jackson: MS Press, 1990; Anette Hoffmann, "Widerspenstige Stimmen/Unruly Voices", Anette Hoffmann (ed.), *What We See*; Anette Hoffmann, "Verbale Riposte: Wilfred Tjiuezas Performances von omitandu als Entgegnungen zum Rassenmodell Hans Lichteneckers", Iris Dressler and Hans D. Christ (eds.), *Acts of Voicing,* Stuttgart: Hatje Cantz, 2014; Anette Hoffmann, "Listening to Sound Archives: Introduction to Edited Section", *Social Dynamics* 41 (1), 2015: *Special Section Listening to Sound Archives*; Anette Hoffmann and Phindezwa Mnyaka, "Hearing Voices in the Archive", *ibid.*; Britta Lange, "'Denken sie selbst über die Sache nach': Tonaufnahmen in deutschen Gefangenenlagern des Ersten Weltkriegs'", Margit Berner, Anette Hoffmann and Britta Lange, *Sensible Sammlungen: Aus dem anthropologischen Depot,* Hamburg: Philo Fine Arts, 2011; Britta Lange, "South Asian Soldiers and German Academics: Anthropological, Linguistic and Musicological Field Studies in Prison Camps", Ravi Ahuja, Heike Liebau and Franziska Roy (eds.), *'When the War Began, We Heard of Several Kings': South Asian Prisoners in World War I Germany,* Delhi: Social Science Press, 2011; Britta Lange, *Die Wiener Forschungen an Kriegsgefangenen 1915-1918: Anthropologische und ethnographische Verfahren im Lager,* Vienna: OAW Verlag, 2013; Artur Simon (ed.), *Das Berliner Phonogramm-Archiv 1900–2000: Sammlungen der traditionellen Musik der Welt,* Berlin: Verlag für Wissenschaft und Bildung, 2000; Burkhardt Stangl, *Ethnologie im Ohr: Die Wirkungsgeschichte des Phonographen,* Vienna: WUV Verlag, 2000; Jonathan Sterne, *The Audible Past: Cultural Origins of Sound Reproduction,* Durham: Duke University Press, 2003.

19 See Britta Lange, *Gefangene Stimmen: Tonaufnahmen von Kriegsgefangenen aus dem Lautarchiv, 1915-1918,* Berlin: Kadmos Verlag, 2020; Anette Hoffmann, *Knowing by Ear: Listening to voice recordings with African prisoners of war in German Camps (1915–1918),*

as examples of speech or music, for example in phonogram archives in Vienna (since 1899), in Berlin (since 1900), but also in St. Petersburg (since 1903), Paris (since 1911) and in many other places.[20] Often recorded outside of Europe for archives in Europe, these acoustic documents are rarely held in institutions in the countries where they were produced.[21] They are thus not known and not available in the regions where historians would be able to identify the specific events the speakers may have addressed, where potential researchers would have the linguistic competence to engage with the performed texts, where words would be heard and understood by listeners who could identify genres of speech and song, where the performative use of voice would make sense to audiences, and where narratives and songs could be connected to a historical repertoire.

In Germany, specific genres of orature were rarely identified, and thus do not appear in archival indexes. An example is a recording with Mohamed Nur, who was a civilian internee of World War I in Germany, which is held at the *Lautarchiv* in Berlin. Perhaps asked by German linguists to perform a "traditional" song, the Somali intellectual presented fragments of poetry that belong to a known body of oral texts, which has been identified as part of a specific historical debate in Somalia.[22] Yet, the index of the *Lautarchiv* in Berlin was and is organized according to colonial nomenclature and ethnic categories. As a result, this rare recording, which holds fragments of a historical debate, sank like a stone. What researchers could not or did not care to know ceased to exist as text and will remain silent, unless researchers turn to close listening.[23]

Durham: Duke University Press, forthcoming.

20 Britta Lange, "Archiv", Daniel Morat and Hansjakob Ziemer (eds.), *Handbuch Sound: Geschichte - Begriffe - Ansätze*, Stuttgart: Metzler 2018.

21 An important exception to this is recordings produced during the so-called *Völkerschauen*, for example in Berlin. Languages and music of the people who performed in these shows in the colonial metropolis were recorded acoustically – see recordings labelled "Archive" plus country names in Ziegler, 2006, p. 80-100. While many of the performers did not stay in Europe, their recordings were kept in the *Phonogramm-Archiv* in Berlin. The situation in the USA is different. Recordings were produced there with Native Americans, and these were also stored in the USA, which makes them more readily accessible to speakers of the languages in which they were recorded. In South Africa, the ILAM archive in Grahamstown holds historical recordings from South Africa, as well as from other African countries.

22 Hoffmann, *Knowing by Ear*.

23 See https://www.re-mapping.eu/de/erinnerungsorte/text/reisende-sollten-unterstutzt-werden-nicht-belastigt-oder-gar-bedroht, accessed January 2021.

In this way, historical recordings that spoke to (then recent) colonial history, or addressed what was then the colonial present directly, did not enter the archival record as contemporary commentary. In sound archives, words and sentences, stories, accounts and songs, which were always articulated for the recordings, never accidentally preserved, and certainly not "collected", often remain acoustically present, yet have become absent in several ways: They were rarely translated or transcribed. Their content does not feature in catalogues and registers, because the cataloguing of the recordings either does not reflect their meaning or does so incorrectly, and because the search terms according to which they are arranged continue to correspond to those of colonial knowledge production.[24]

Another example of this loss of words due to the inability or unwillingness to hear historical comment or critique, is a recording with another civilian internee of World War I, Stephan Bischoff, who had migrated to Germany around 1910 from what was then the Gold Coast. At the behest of the linguist Carl Meinhof, Stephan Bischoff presented a fable that addresses a specific moment of colonial violence, namely the destruction of a shrine in Kete Krachi in 1913 by the German colonial military. In the written register of the *Lautarchiv*, the fable is listed as "The Story of the 5000 Monkeys."[25]

The ongoing digitization of historical sound recordings produced since the end of the 19th century has added to the mobility of acoustic collections. Digital files travel more easily than wax cylinders, which facilitates the work of translation and interpretation outside the archives. Yet the existence of thousands of acoustic recordings in European archives still remains mostly unknown in the countries of their origin, or those where their speakers came from. Sporadic restitutions in recent years – in the form of CDs or digital sound files – have not altered this situation structurally.[26] Despite repeated promises to the contrary, most European

---

24 See, for example, the collection of the Berlin *Lautarchiv*, https://www.sammlungen.
hu-berlin.de/objekte/lautarchiv/13246/, or the *Phonogramm-Archiv* in Berlin, http://
www.smb-digital.de/eMuseumPlus, accessed January 2021.

25 "Die Geschichte von den 5000 Affen", see Hoffmann, *Knowing By Ear.*

26 Méhéza Kalibani, "Kolonialer Tinnitus: Das belastende Geräusch des Kolonialismus",
Geschichte in Wissenschaft und Unterrricht 9/10, 2021; Miguel A. Garcfa, "Sound Archives under Suspicion", Susanne Ziegler, Ingrid Åkesson, Gerda Lechleitner and Susana Gardo (eds.), *Historical Sources of Ethnomusicology in Contemporary Debate*, Cambridge: Cambridge Scholars, 2017; Anette Hoffmann, "Listening to Sound Archives".

sound archives have not proactively or systematically taken on their responsibility for the acoustic traces of European colonial heritage, which is not merely a heritage of objects, but also a heritage of continued practices.[27] Discarding or ignoring the spoken or sung words of those who often also had been subjected to anthropometric examinations, who were photographed, measured and described, thus followed the order of colonial knowledge production, in which those who were marked and objectified by means of racializing practices, were often visually represented but rarely appeared as speakers. And while these speakers had not been asked to give an account of themselves, they sometimes did. The echoes of their voices, in the acoustic but also the political sense – which are often not congruent – have rarely been heard in public.[28] Because the recorded, archived, preserved, often already digitized words are difficult to find in the archives, they are also not accessible for the writing of historiographies, for studying the practices of colonial epistemological practices, or when seeking to include the enunciative positions of those who were subjected to racializing studies.

For more than three decades, questions around the crafting of historiographies on the basis of the colonial archive, that is, based on the texts of colonial officials, linguists and anthropologists, the reports of the military, the narratives of missionaries and adventurers, the mass of objectifying illustrations, and in relation to the question of the accessibility of subaltern speech positions have been discussed. In this debate, which has been active in Southern Africa and in Southeast Asia long before it was

27 For a project that does take on this responsibility see Barbara Titus and meLê Yamomo, "The Persistent Refrain of the Colonial Archival Logic/Colonial Entanglements and Sonic Transgressions: Sounding out the Jaap Kunst Collection", *World of Music* 10 (1) 2021.

28 On voice as a ubiquitous metaphor for political participation, but also as a cultural and physical phenomenon, I have written elsewhere. See Hoffmann and Mnyaka, "Hearing Voices in the Archive"; Hoffmann, "Listening to Sound Archives"; Hoffmann, "Verbale Riposte". See also Mladen Dolar, *A Voice and Nothing More*, Cambridge and London: MIT Press 2006; Adriana Cavero, "For More Than One Voice", Thomas Trummer (ed.), *Voice and Void*, New York: The Aldrich Contemporary Art Museum 2007; and Krämer (eds.), *Voice*; Amanda Weidmann, "Voice", David Novak and Matt Sakakeeny (eds.), *Keywords in Sound*, Durham and London: Duke University Press, 2015; Jennifer Stoever, *The Sonic Color Line: Race and the Cultural Politics of Listening*, New York: New York University Press, 2016.

picked up in Europe, the sound archives of colonial knowledge production are yet to be included.[29]

In the discussion around colonial knowledge production, the archive has largely remained silent acoustically. Apart from the consequences of archival processes and word-deafness, other reasons for this disinterest in acoustic archives include the longstanding academic preference for written sources, which led to the neglect of (for instance) colonial photographic archives until some decades ago. Another reason is the poor accessibility of sound archives, for instance from countries where oral transmission of knowledge is considered relevant and vital.

Unlike photographic and textual collections, historical sound recordings are yet to be understood as sources of colonial history. In contrast to the often more accessible texts and photographs of the colonial archive, acoustic documents also reach the public sphere – museums or art exhibitions, for example – less frequently, and when they are played, they are mostly treated as acoustic wallpaper, that is, ambient sound without text. A recent example of this is an audio recording of the prisoner-of-war, Massaud bin Mohammed bin Salah, who was also recorded by linguists in a prison camp in Germany during the First World War I. The recording was played in the exhibition *Deutscher Kolonialismus, Fragmente seiner Geschichte und Gegenwart* (October 2016—May 2017)[30] at the *Deutsches Historisches Museum* (German Historical Museum) in Berlin. The sound recording was acoustically present in the exhibition and a depiction of the speaker was shown, but his spoken text, which had been translated and published by August Klingenheben and Carl Meinhof in 1929 already, did not feature in the exhibition. As a consequence, Massaud bin Mohamed bin Salah's spoken words were not available as a source of colonial history, in the biggest

29 As one of the major hubs for this debate and research around archive, see the website of the Archive and Public Culture Research Initiative at the University of Cape Town, http://www.apc.uct.ac.za/, accessed January 2021. See also Gayatri C. Spivak, "Can the Subaltern Speak?", C. Nelson and L. Grossberg (eds.), *Marxism and the Interpretation of Cultures*, Basingstoke: Macmillan, 1988; Gayatri C. Spivak, *A Critique of Postcolonial Reason: Toward a History of the Vanishing Present*, Cambridge, Massachusetts and London: Harvard University Press, 1999; Lalu, *The Deaths of Hintsa*; Prakash, "The Impossibility of Subaltern History"; Leslie Witz and Ciraj Rassool, "Making Histories", *Kronos* 34, 2008; Carolyn Hamilton and Nessa Leibhammer (eds.), *Tribing and Untribing the Archive*, Pietermaritzburg, UKZN Press, 2016.

30 The title of the exhibition translates as: "German Colonialism, Fragments of its History and Presence".

exhibition on German colonialism in a German museum to date.[31] Massaud bin Mohamed bin Salah thus remained in the inarticulate position assigned to him by colonial knowledge production a century ago. What he said became ambient sound in this exhibition; it could not be heard or understood as a comment on German colonialism in Germany in 2016. Whereas lists of body measurements, plaster casts of faces or body parts, racializing descriptions and illustrations have increasingly been mined from archives or from collections of particular disciplines, and do appear in critical artworks and curatorial presentations in the public domain, historical sound recordings only recently have begun to leave the seclusion of the archive.[32]

Limiting categorizations of spoken texts as linguistic specimens are examples of enduring historical figurations that have constrained their ability to communicate content. These historical figurations seem difficult to shake off. Their persistence precludes hearing sound recordings as semantically meaningful, spoken, sung, historical texts in the present. Disciplinary sequestration also sundered objects that came from the same expedition. Following the logic of disciplines, objects were ordered into separate categories, which included ethnological objects, anthropometric data, casts, photographs, acoustic collections and human remains, and were then subsequently held in distinct institutions. For the collection that goes back to the Kalahari expedition of the Austrian anthropologist Ru-

---

31 *Lautabteilung der Preußischen Staatsbibliothek* 1929, "Mandara, aufgezeichnet von Carl Meinhof, bearbeitet von August Klingenheben", *Phonetische Platten und Umschriften* No. 48. The language described by August Klingenheben and Carl Meinhof as "Mandara" seems to belong to the Biu-Mandara dialect cluster. It is not clear to me exactly which language it is according to recent nomenclature.

32 Recent examples of the artistic and curatorial engagement with historical images of "racial typification" in German-speaking countries include Rajkamal Kahlon's exhibition *Staying with Trouble* at the *Weltmuseum* in Vienna (25.10.2017–8.1.2019) and the exhibition *Rassismus: Die Erfindung von Menschrassen,* curated by Susanne Wernsing at the *Deutsches Hygienemuseum* in Dresden 2018/19; see also Susanne Wernsing, Christian Geulen and Klaus Vogel (eds.), *Rassismus: Die Erfindung von Menschenrassen,* Göttingen: Wallstein Verlag, 2018; Naika Foroutan *et al., Das Phantom „Rasse": Zur Geschichte und Wirkungsmacht von Rassismus,* Cologne: Böhlau, 2018. For recent work on/with historical sound recordings from German archives see for instance meLê Yamomo's *Echoing Europe* (https://ballhausnaunynstrasse.de/play/echoing_europe_-__postcolonial_reverberations/); the work of *Listening at Pungwe* (Memory Biwa and Robert Machiri) https://listeningatpungwe.wordpress.com/; and Heiner Goebbels' *A House of Call,* https://www.ensemble-modern.com/de/projekte/aktuell/heiner-goebbels-2020; among others, all accessed February 2022.

dolf Pöch, which will be the subject of the next three chapters of this book, this means that Pöch's spoils were distributed among five Viennese institutions: the *Naturhistorisches Museum* (Natural History Museum), the *Weltmuseum* (World Museum), the *Department für Evolutionäre Anthropologie* (Department of Evolutionary Anthropology) at the University of Vienna, the *Phonogrammarchiv* (Phonogram Archive at the Austrian Academy of Sciences) and the *Filmarchiv* Austria (Film Archive Austria).

In the course of distributing objects to various institutions, crucial connections between the now-separated objects were eradicated. In the present, this historical segregation means that images as well as objects which relate to specific recorded speakers may exist, yet are not known in the sound archives. In the case of the recordings from Namibia in 1931, held in the Berlin *Phonogramm-Archiv*, in which speakers comment on the practice of making casts of their faces and bodies, no information was available in 2007 on the whereabouts of the collection of casts to which these recordings referred.[33]

As mentioned above, the incomplete, incorrect, or missing documentation of the recordings and speakers often goes back to the recording situation. Missing or sketchy documentation, compounded by the separation of different objects from a collection, bedevils the study of acoustic documents of colonial history, as it disallows the reconstruction of recording situations, and the identification of speakers. The identification of discursive fragments in the present thus often depends on the possibility of reassembling collections across archives. By "reassembling", I mean a systematic reassociation or reconnection of photographs, texts or objects that relate to historical sound recordings and speakers. Reassembling a collection[34] expands our understanding of what was said or sung, and may allow researchers to retrieve previously obscured aspects of the recording situation. A fundamental part of my work on historical sound recordings

33   Anette Hoffmann, "Widerspenstige Stimmen/Unruly Voices", Anette Hoffmann (ed.), *What We See*; Anette Hoffmann, "Finding Words (of Anger)", *ibid.*; Anette Hoffmann, "Glaubwürdige Inszenierungen: Die Produktion von Abformungen in der Polizeistation in Keetmanshoop im August 1931", Berner, Hoffmann and Lange, *Sensible Sammlungen*, "'Oh meine Schester, mein Rücken brennt sehr und ich bin machtlos!' Voice Over I, Haneb", *ibid.*; Anette Hoffmann, "Wie ein Hund in einem Fangeisen schreien: Voice Over II, Kanaje", *ibid.*

34   See Rodney Harrison, Sarah Byrne and Anne Clarke (eds.), *Reassembling the Collection: Ethnographic Museums and Indigenous Agency*, Santa Fe: SAR Press, 2014.

therefore consists of seeking to re-establish relationships between speakers and archival objects, tracing networks of collectors, researchers and archives, but also of reconstructing historical practices that led to preservation or loss. In many cases I have had to leave the sound archive in order to better understand its collections.

The ongoing digitization of historical sound recordings has diminished barriers to accessibility, but by no means removed them altogether. At present, it remains difficult to search German sound archives online because indexes are not available digitally, are generally not user-friendly, or exist only in German, which is an obstruction especially for researchers from the countries where many of the recordings came from. These language barriers result from the politics of colonial knowledge production with its inherently unidirectional flow of information, according to the logic of which recordings were often produced outside of Europe and then archived in European metropolises. Incorrect colonial or racist terminologies, most of which continue to be used after digitization, make it difficult to find relevant recordings. [35] In addition, most registers of sound archives to date do not document the coercive context of the recordings, which often took place in prison camps (the recordings of the *Königlich Preußische Phonographische Kommission, Lautarchiv,* Berlin, 1915—1918), prisons, pass offices and police stations (the recordings of Felix von Luschan in South Africa in 1905 and of Hans Lichtenecker in Namibia in 1931, at the *Phonogramm-Archiv* Berlin) or in other coercive colonial situations (the collection of Rudolf Pöch – see chapters 2–4 of this book). While often absent from the written record, echoes of their recording situations *are* often audible in the recordings themselves. This means that comments or fragments of discursive formations that do not exist in any other form have been acoustically preserved.

By means of close listening and retranslation, it often becomes clear that those to whom colonial knowledge production did not grant a position to comment or criticize, whose utterances were not heard as part of

---

35 A drastic, but by no means isolated, example is the designation of speakers as *"Lippenneger(innen)"* (lip negroes), which definitely dates back to the recordist Meinulf Küsters (1930), and which appears in Ziegler's catalogue of the wax cylinders of the Berlin *Phonogramm-Archiv* and was probably adopted unaltered from there for the online database of the *Staatliche Museen zu Berlin* (National Museums of Berlin). See *Die Wachszylinder des Berliner Phonogramm-Archivs,* 2006 p. 183.

a conversation or even as meaningful speech acts, nevertheless did assume the position of speakers. At times, this meant that speakers would deliberately ignore the power relations of the field of knowledge production. These moments of rejection can be heard as a form of critique that involves assuming a position of speaking that responds to the situation of colonial knowledge production without being asked to do so.[36] Echoes of these moments have entered the colonial archive as recordings. This is of significance for decolonial historiographies when, as in the case of the aforementioned so-called Kalahari recordings, unexpected speaking positions surface with (re)translation, which show that speakers did emphatically criticize the practices of the anthropologist or articulate their fear of speaking.[37] Close listening, together with retranslation, thus attends to the asymmetries of power that resound in a recording (see chapter 2 and chapter 4).

Speech acts that, upon close listening, exceed the logics and limitations of their artefactualization as linguistic specimens[38] have surfaced in *every* acoustic collection I have studied so far. Examples include the audio recording with World War I prisoner, Abdulaye Niang (Wünsdorf camp, 1917), who asked not to be deported to another camp; a recording with Petrus Goliath in Witpütz (Namibia, 1931), who gave an account of the suffocating experience of having his face cast with a hot, wax-like mass; and the recording with the Naro speaker |Kxara in Ghanzi (1908), who angrily demands his knife which the anthropologist had probably appropriated for his collection (see chapter 4).[39] These and other speech acts may not have been understood by the recordists in the moment of re-

---

36   Ruth Sonderegger speaks of *Gleichheitsforderung*, a request to be treated as equal, in chapter 5 of her book *Vom Leben der Kritik: Kritische Praktiken und die Notwendigkeit ihrer geopolitischen Situierung*, Wien: Zaglossus, 2019. This request can be heard in a recording I discuss in chapter 4 of this book.

37   Anette Hoffmann, "Finding Words (of Anger)"; "'Oh meine Schwester, mein Rücken brennt sehr, und ich bin machtlos!'"; "'Wie ein Hund in einem Fangeisen schreien'"; "Kolonialität", Daniel Morat and Hansjakob Ziemer (eds.), *Handbuch Sound: Geschichte – Begriffe – Ansätze*, Stuttgart: Metzler 2018; Britta Lange, "'Denken sie selbst über die Sache nach'"; "Poste Restante, and Messages in Bottles: Sound Recordings of Indian Prisoners in the First World War", *Social Dynamics* 41 (1), 2015: *Special Section Listening to Sound Archives*; Ruth Sonderegger, "What One Does (Not) Hear".

38   Jan Blommaert, "Artefactual ideologies and the textual production of African languages", *Language and Communication* 28, 2008.

39   Hoffmann, "Finding Words (of Anger)".

cording, and they often have not been translated, even when translators were present. In many cases, the semantic content and genre of these recordings were deemed irrelevant by the researcher. The urgent plea of Abdulaye Niang from Senegal not to be deported to another camp was recorded during the course of the extensive linguistic survey by the *Königlich Preußische Phonographische Kommission* in German prison camps.[40] It was registered as a "narrative" and has been archived as such.[41] The vague designation *Erzählung* (narrative) in this case probably points to the fact that the recording philologist Wilhelm Doegen did not notice Niang's appeal, or chose to ignore it. Consequently, for about 100 years, the recording in the Berlin *Lautarchiv* was not identified as a historical document of the deportation of African soldiers to Romania, until we listened to it again, and until it was re-translated by Serigne Matar Niang.[42] On their visit to Wünsdorf camp before Niang was moved to Romania, Austrian anthropologists examined and measured Abdulaye Niang's body, and they photographed him. Mugshots, which exposed his naked chest, together with the results of anthropometric measurements of his body, appeared in two publications which presented Niang as "Wolof". He was thus presented as a particular racial or ethnic type constructed by the researchers.[43] In Doegen's 1941 publication, another photograph of Niang's was included without his name. What Abdulaye Niang had said was not available in any of these publications, nor did it appear elsewhere for over a century. In the order of colonial knowledge production, followed by archiving, and subsequent publication, Abdulaye Niang was thus not granted a position to speak; his words were swallowed in the collection of linguistic record-

40 Hoffmann, *Knowing by Ear.*
41 The recording practice of the commission has been researched and described in great detail by Britta Lange, see *Gefangene Stimmen.* See also Irene Hilden, "Who sang this song? An acoustic testimony between self-empowerment and object status", Anna-Maria Brandstetter and Vera Hierholzer (eds.), *Nicht nur Raubkunst! Sensible Dinge in Museen und universitären Sammlungen,* Mainz: Mainz University Press, 2018; Hoffmann, "Echoes of the Great War"; Hoffman and Mnyaka, "Hearing Voices in the Archive".
42 Hoffmann, *Knowing by Ear.*
43 Josef Weninger, *Eine morphologisch-anthropologische Studie: Durchgeführt an 100 westafrikanischen Negern, als Beitrag zur Anthropologie von Afrika,* Vienna: *Verlag der Anthropologischen Gesellschaft* 1926; Wilhelm Doegen, *Unsere Gegner damals und heute: Engländer und Franzosen und ihre fremdrassigen Hilfsvölker in der Heimat, an der Front und in Gefangenschaft im Weltkriege und im jetzigen Kriege, Großdeutschlands koloniale Sendung,* Berlin, 1941.

ings with prisoners of World War I in the Berlin *Lautarchiv*, where they were filed as examples of the Wolof language.[44] Decades later, in 1941, the German musicologist Fritz Bose revisited the recordings with Abdulaye Niang, only to listen to them with the attempt to construe a connection between voice and fascist concepts of race. Like Doegen before him, Bose made no attempt to understand Abdulaye Niang's spoken text. The speaker's urgent plea was of no use for the research on voice and race; it thus remained unmentioned.[45]

Apart from carrying words which were omitted from the archival record, acoustic recordings transmit the excess of voice, including changes in tone, whispers and sometimes ambivalent, non-textual sounds such as laughter, the clearing of a throat, or coughing.[46] These prosodic utterances only exist acoustically. Once listeners attend to these acoustic traces, they may radically shift the meaning of what was said, conveying irony, uncertainty, or anger.

In archival registers, but also in the heroic tales that institutions still tell, recordists have been called "collectors", even though sound recordings have always been produced and were never collected.[47] In the documentation of the archive, voice was swallowed together with words; what it can communicate performatively was dismissed in favour of preserving linguistic specimens. First translations of historical sound recordings in the present, or their informed re-translation, often show that the archival designations given to the recordings scarcely correspond with the actual acoustic objects, that is, the speech acts, narratives, songs or statements they were meant to document. One of the recurring, sometimes

---

44 The recordings with the Wolof speaker Abdulaye Niang are discussed in the first chapter of my monograph about the sound recordings with African prisoners-of-war kept in the Berlin *Lautarchiv*. They were first translated by Serigne Matar Niang in 2013 (*Knowing by Ear*).

45 *Ibid.*

46 In the course of my exhibition *Was Wir Sehen: Stimmen, Bilder*, which took place in the summer of 2012 at the *Pergamon Palais* of the Humboldt University Berlin, Britta Lange presented her *Flüsterspur* ("Whispering Track"), a sound installation consisting of exclusively non-semantic human sound utterances heard on historical sound recordings from the *Lautarchiv*. See https://anettehoffmann.com/what-we-see-2009-2013/, accessed January 2022. See also Anette Hoffmann, Regina Sarreiter and Britta Lange, *Was Wir Sehen: Bilder, Stimmen, Rauschen: Zur Kritik anthropometrischen Sammelns*, Basel: Basler Afrika Bibliographien, 2012.

47 Sterne, *The Audible Past*.

disturbing, echoes of colonial knowledge production are the recordists' announcements. These announcements, which elsewhere I have called "acoustic tags" of recordings,[48] served to identify the spoken text and the language, which followed. This was seen as necessary, particularly for recordings in non-European languages. Yet this spoken tag, which is part of the sonic composition of the recording, does not appear in the description and labelling of a recording. Thus, when the adventurer Hans Lichtenecker barked, *"Achtung, Aufnahme!"* (Attention, recording!) into the funnel of a phonograph at the police station in Keetmanshoop in the southern winter of 1931, the recording preserved his authoritarian demeanour. But Lichtenecker's announcement, which speaks of the recording situation, does not appear in the written label of wax cylinder 33 of this collection in the *Phonogramm-Archiv;* it exists exclusively in the acoustic document.[49] The recent digitization of the collection has not altered this. Instead it has confirmed the understanding of recordings as predefined objects, for instance language examples. In this case, the words and voice of the person who recorded were swallowed in the documentation, because these do not feature as parts of the object or historical artefact. Neither is the recording understood as the soundtrack of an epistemological practice. As a consequence, this and other recordings are not described as composite sonic documents in the index of the archive.

Even more astounding is the example of a recording that will be discussed in the third chapter of this book, in which the Austrian anthropologist Rudolf Pöch speaks a crude mix of Dutch, Afrikaans, English and German. This recording cannot be found in the tracks listed on the CD of the digitized collection published in 2003, nor is it listed in the index of the *Phonogrammarchiv* in Vienna. Again, the predefinition of objects of interest or study precluded the inclusion of the soundtrack of knowledge production from indexes and catalogues. In this way, practices of colonial knowledge production and archiving have created a durable incommensurability between sound and text documents. As a result, what can be heard still cannot be read.

48   Hoffmann, "Listening to Sound Archives".

49   Collection Hans Lichtenecker, *Phonogramm-Archiv* Berlin, see Anette Hoffmann, "'Achtung Aufnahme!' Akustische Spuren kolonialer Wissensproduktion", Iris Edenheiser and Larissa Förster (eds.), *Museumsethnologie: Eine Einführung: Theorien - Debatten - Praktiken*, Berlin: Dietrich Reimer Verlag, 2019.

Accordingly, historical sound recordings now offer a hitherto barely noted wealth of sources: spoken commentaries that had fallen silent in the colonial archive can be revisited; we can listen in on the historical moment of recording. Voiceovers that comment on colonial knowledge production from the perspective of those who were subjected to its epistemic practices have survived as acoustic documents.[50] At times, the instructions of the recordists can be heard, or the presence of listeners is audible, which may provide information about the situation in which the recording took place.

CLOSE LISTENING

In addition to the systematic reconstruction or reassociation of archival objects which were historically connected to the recordings, I understand my approach to these acoustic sources as "close listening".[51] Close listening is a practice of listening that pays attention to *everything that is audible* on a recording: voice(s), background noises, clearing of the throat and coughing, laughter, pauses, the announcements of the recordists, the rumble of the phonograph, as well as the intonation of what was said.[52] Close listening attends to all acoustic signals and may thus, for example, shift listeners' attention away from the limitations of a statement that was indexed as an example of speech, towards speech as a performative, expressive form of utterance. Close listening attends to the tone of voice of the person(s) recorded and to audible hints of the presence of listeners who may have been addressed by the speaker.

As a practice of listening to acoustic archival documents, this often means listening collectively. Close listening may not alter historical subject positions; nor will it enable listeners to find answers to the questions

50 Hoffmann, "'Oh meine Schwester, mein Rücken brennt sehr und ich bin machtlos!'", p. 129.
51 As a first approach, the idea of *close listening* emerged in conversations with Britta Lange while we were teaching a seminar on sound archives at Humboldt University Berlin in summer 2012. In a series of workshops which I organized at the Archive and Public Culture Research Initiative at the University of Cape Town, I was able to further develop the method of close listening together with the participants. I would like to thank Britta Lange, Thokozani Mhlambi, Rosemary Lombard, Memory Biwa, Katleho Shoro, Carolyn Hamilton, Thuthuka Sibisi, Philip Miller, Niklas Zimmer, Renate Meyer, Debra Pryor, Michael Nixon, Anthony Sloan, George Mahashe, and Joanne Bloch for the immensely productive discussions and for listening collectively. See Hoffmann, *Kolonialgeschichte hören*; "Close Listening"; Lange, *Gefangene Stimmen*.
52 Hoffmann, "Listening to Sound Archives".

we have in the present. It attends to, but cannot not restore, fragmented texts or faint audio signals. However, close listening in the present, together with informed translation which can identify genres, engages with the performativity of voice and may challenge the figuring of acoustically documented speech acts according to disciplinary interests, for example, linguistics. In the first place, close listening means actual *listening*, instead of reading the index and/or the transcriptions the archive provides. Seeking to know by ear may retrieve the significance of preserved speech acts or songs retrospectively, undoing their former artefactualization as linguistic examples by focusing on what was actually said or sung, and what non-verbal expression the voice may have carried. Close listening demonstrates, as I will show in the following chapters, that many speakers did not articulate linguistic examples. They communicated, or made an attempt to do so. Hearing acoustic recordings as speech, utterances, or song may thus refigure sound recordings as historical traces.

Many of the configurations that come with recording are irreversible, for example the abbreviation of narratives to the duration of one wax cylinder of two to three minutes' playing time. This did not merely follow from technical requirements: a story could conceivably have been recorded in full length, on several cylinders. The asymmetrical power relations, which were virtually etched into each of the recordings with African POWs, were acknowledged *and* disregarded by Abdulaye Niang, who used the moment of recording to petition against the prisoners' deportation.[53] His recording, and all other language recordings with prisoners-of-war in the Berlin *Lautarchiv,* exist solely because linguists were interested in recording languages and dialects. While we can hear Abdulaye Niang's urgent plea today, because he decided to articulate it, his utterance was nevertheless limited to the duration of an Edison wax cylinder. This formatting of his speech recording cannot be altered by another way of listening.

The systematic and durable concealment of the modes of production of many recordings – in prison camps, during guerrilla wars, in police and military stations, in colonized regions – has led to decontextualization, not only of the semantic content of what was said. These modes of knowledge production often also influenced how something could

---

53   On the irreversible marks the archive leaves on objects and documents, see Ann Laura
      Stoler, *Along the Archival Grain,* p. 8.

be said and what the performativity of voice may have transmitted. Often recording situations and particular requests prompted speech acts or asked for performances in particular forms and genres. Yet the recordings were subsequently archived without documenting the researcher's request, which would explain their existence. Yet the echo to the question may have remained in the speakers' response.

The focus of linguists on grammatical structures and the pronunciation of specific languages also led to a suspension of the expressivity of the speaking or singing voice in later publications. In the 42nd publication of the *Lautbibliothek* in Berlin with the title *"Xhosa in Südafrica" aufgenommen von Carl Meinhof and bearbeitet von Archibald Tucker"*, the linguist Tucker describes the chants of a prisoner of war as "meaningless ejaculations" *(bedeutungslose Ergüsse)*.[54] The singer's name was registered as Josef Twanumbee (more likely: Ntwanumbi) in the files of the *Lautarchiv*. His name was not mentioned in this publication, yet Tucker noted that the recordings were produced by Carl Meinhof in 1917. Neither the fact that this happened in the so-called *Engländer Lager* in Ruhleben, which was a camp where British subjects were interned during the war, nor that the person recorded was an internee, surfaces in the text. In one of his songs, the singer interweaves his earlier experience of initiation in South Africa, during which boys were isolated for a certain period of time and had to pass a series of tests and trials, with his experience in the prisoner-of-war camp in Germany. This intricate performative articulation, which makes use of words and voice to adapt this particular genre to the speaker's situation, has become incomprehensible without its context.[55] The dramatic performance of the chant and the immense sadness his voice transmits are not mentioned in the transcription, which ignores the ordeal of the singer.

As in this case, colonial linguistic treatments of sound recordings often undercut the performative potential of the singing or speaking voice, which continues to resound in the acoustic document, for example, in wordless chants or in performances of poetry. The melody of voice, together with its performative properties, cannot be transferred to a transcribed text. In this publication they became "meaningless ejaculations"

---

54 The title translates as "Xhosa in South Africa: recorded by Prof. Dr. C. Meinhof, edited by Dr. A. N. Tucker", published in the series of the *Lautbibliothek* in 1936.
55 Hoffmann and Mnyaka, "Hearing Voices in the Archive".

because their expressive meaning was of no use for linguists, who were interested in *langue*, and not in *parole*. Particularly with regard to audible changes of pitch, which often express derision or irony, the omission of prosodic expression leads to a loss or shift in meaning in the transcription. Close listening, together with informed retranslations of acoustic documents, may retrieve the expressivity of the communicating voice. This, too, highlights the potential of historical sound recordings, which has received too little attention thus far: what cannot be read in the minutes, registers, reports, and other written documentation produced by the recordists is often still audible. The recordings discussed in the following chapters are marked with an ear symbol ℈ on first appearance. The list of links which connect to the site of the Austrian Academy of Science can be found on page 152.

Because of this significant difference between a transcription and a recording, between what has been said *about* a speaking person subjected to examination, and what was said *by* someone whose speech or music was the object of study, or who themselves had been the object of study, the question of subaltern speech positions and texts in the colonial archive presents itself anew in historical sound recordings. The question is thus whether, after the inclusion of historical sound recordings as part of the colonial archive, the argument that the colonial archive has systematically erased *all* subaltern speech positions still holds. Gyan Prakash's argument that traces of subaltern actions, their presence and critique are most likely to be found in the interstices of discourse (for example, of the colonial administration), in the voids and blind spots of the archive, arguably speaks to or for an archive which consists solely of texts and images. I suggest that the inclusion of thousands of sound documents not previously perceived as historical sources explodes our current understanding of the colonial archive.[56] Premesh Lalu's notion of the untraceability or fundamental unreconstructability of subaltern speaking positions in the colonial archive seems valid for textual archives and, perhaps more limitedly, for archival images.[57] Yet this argument, that the colonial archive always directs researchers according to its own inherent logic, may be the precise reason that sound recordings have rarely been heard as historical

56   Prakash, "Subaltern Studies as Postcolonial Criticism", p. 1482.
57   Lalu, *The Deaths of Hintsa*, p. 63.

statements and sources. In keeping with the logic of colonial knowledge production, the acoustically documented speech acts of those who were systematically denied a position to speak, based on racial constructions, have been filed away until the present as examples of speech and music or, at best, as folkloric narratives. In accordance with the order of written documentation and the disciplinary separation of archival objects, acoustic documents recorded by linguists as examples of speech have thus been overlooked as textual sources of colonial history. This does not mean, however, that they do not speak. Rather, as I will show in what follows, subaltern speaking positions, together with comments and critique, can be found in acoustic collections, even if these were not recorded with the intention to document social history. To this end, it is crucial to distinguish the moment of speaking from the moment of archiving, even if speakers heard in acoustic recordings were recorded with the predefined aim of archiving their spoken texts or songs. While, as Michel-Rolph Trouillot has noted, "in history, power begins at the source,"[58] the process of archiving involves a series of selective activities – the selection of sources, of procedures, but also selections of evidence and relevance.[59] These choices and interests, together with politics of access and practice of conservation, as Carolyn Hamilton has shown, may change over time, which means that archival objects are not static, nor do they stay the same.[60] In fact the missing of words I have identified here only occurs when the recordings have changed already: from specimens of language, to records of colonial knowledge production and carriers of spoken text that can be heard as commentary, accounts and contemporary critique.

Regardless of the intentions of those who recorded, in the situation of acoustic documentation the speakers did not necessarily submit to the ideas and aims of researchers. For example, speakers may have presented assessments of their past, the colonial present and their own position in the moment of recording instead. In other words, speakers often articulated what came to their minds, what they considered to be important, or

---

58   Trouillot, *Silencing the Past*, p. 29.
59   *Ibid.* p. 53.
60   Carolyn Hamilton, "Backstory, Biography, and the Life of the James Stuart Archive", *History in Africa* 38, 2011; and "Forged and Continually Refashioned in the Crucibles of Ongoing Social and Political Life: Archives and Custodial Practices as Subjects of Inquiry", *South African Historical Journal*, 65 (1), 2013.

worthy of conservation, in the moment of speaking. Because speakers had no control over the subsequent order to which their spoken or sung texts were subjected, and because they did not participate in subsequent processes of archiving, their utterances were literally swallowed by the colonial archive.

In collections of historical sound recordings, acoustic voices have been preserved which, even as recorded echo, still convey a more direct trace of what was said than a transcription could deliver. Unlike the report transcribed by a "village scribe" in the mid-19th century, which was then adapted to the conventions of legal testimony, on the basis of which the historian Ranajit Guha attempted to re-read and re-interpret the circumstances of the death of a young woman in the 19th century in his now-canonical text *Chandra's Death* (1987) in the fifth volume of *Subaltern Studies*, historical audio recordings can be revisited and listened to again. The spoken text as a sample of speech may be drastically decontextualized; its content may never have appeared in written documentation, yet in recording, words may have survived in their original sequence, rhythm and tone. The spoken text in an intact recording does not become overwritten by a transcription. The recording itself is not swallowed with its omission from written documentation. This also means that audio recordings such as Abdulaye Niang's do not have to be read *against* the grain so as to detect a speaking position that may not be discoverable in the same way among the images and in the texts of the colonial archive.[61] The argument I am making here with my study of the 1908 sound recordings from the Kalahari, which Rudolf Pöch brought to Vienna, and based on my work on other historical sound collections, is thus directed against the assumption that the colonial archive never allows utterances from subaltern positions, always overwrites them, or systematically disallows their existence.[62]

Listening closely to historical sound recordings holds the potential for a different approach to subaltern speaking positions within colonial power structures for other reasons as well: because speakers were often

61 For a discussion about reading the archive with or against the grain, see Ann Laura Stoler, *Along the Archival Grain*.
62 See Rosalind C. Morris, "Introduction", Rosalind C. Morris (ed.), *Can the Subaltern Speak? Reflections on the History of an Idea*, New York: Columbia University Press, 2010; Spivak, "Can the Subaltern Speak?"; Spivak, "In Response: Looking Back, Looking Forward", *ibid*.

sure they would not be understood; because freedom of speech granted in their cultural context allowed for direct criticism in certain situations, with certain genres and prosodic expressions; because they said what was important to them and not necessarily what researchers wanted to record; and because, for most speakers, moments of speaking were moments of communication and not occasions to present examples of language. Moreover, in the moments of speaking or singing for a recording, speakers often assumed the position of experts who tapped into a rich repertoire of oral expressions unknown to those who operated the recording device. Opacity was, and still is, a feature of specific genres of poetry, for instance in southern Africa. This allowed speakers to encode what they were saying. The recording situation thus often became an opportunity for speakers or singers to communicate with listeners while ensuring that the recordists would not understand them.[63]

Returning to Ranajit Guha's "reading between the lines" as a recuperative practice or as an attempt to probe subaltern positions, which marks at least one of the beginnings of *Subaltern Studies* and was later seen as romanticizing, or too sanguine, I suggest that sound recordings can provide a more direct, though not necessarily *the* direct, access to subaltern enunciative positions. For even if acoustic sources only allow listeners access to the acoustic voice as a political or subjective voice in some cases, the possibility of listening again to aspects of the recording situation remains. The felicitous case of a well-preserved recording allows listeners to check existing transcriptions or questionable translations (see chapters 3 and 4). Thus, instead of reclaiming for historiography, as Guha did, a historical transcription of which the circumstances of writing remain unclear, instead of wondering how accurate a transcription is and what has been left out – the coughing, the laughing, the clearing of throats, the pauses or changes in tone that can convey uncertainty, fear and excitement – audio recordings can be revisited to listen to them as or with speakers of the recorded language. When revisiting a historical recording, close listening also entails discussing genres and the use of voice, trying to discern whether a narrative is or was part of a particular repertoire or historical discur-

---

63   Leroy Vail and Landeg White, *Power and the Praise Poem: Southern African Voices in History*, London: James Currey, 1991; Luise White, *Speaking with Vampires: Rumor and History in Colonial Africa*, Berkeley and Los Angeles: University of California Press, 2000; Hoffmann, "Verbal Riposte."

sive formation. Close listening is therefore often a collaborative practice in which sound recordings are heard together with (other) speakers of the language(s) in question and discussed with experts in that language.

Although sound collections have barely been included in the long debate around the colonial archive, their specificity does not place them outside of the logics and practical figurations of the archive.[64] While in many cases words can be recovered and revived at least as distant echoes of a conversation – as discursive elements or fragments of narratives – I do not claim that to unearth this soundtrack could entirely disclose the experience of someone on the receiving end of epistemic violence. Nor can it reassemble the atomized bodies of anthropometric images and repair the archival trace of people who were once studied and now appear as objectified figures. Instead, close listening attends to polyphonic, belated echoes, which resound with the coloniality of the recordists and resonate with practices of recording, together with the echo of the speech acts of those who were recorded. What close listening in the present can undo is the reduction of spoken texts to their designation as linguistic examples. When combined with the work of reassembling the personal traces of speakers, close listening adds to the complexity of what can be known of speakers who may have left traces in more than one medium. It may allow us to perceive distortions caused by racializing representations.

Altogether, my approach to close listening is the result of a shift in interest, which allowed me to hear historical recordings as acoustic documents of colonial knowledge production. This strategic move to revisit the archive as a listener is also a change of the terms of engagement in the present.[65] In my research this led to an understanding of spoken texts once produced as examples of speech or music as semantically meaningful utterances. And, while strategies in the present cannot undo the historical *mèsentente* of the recording situation, speakers can be met in terms of their utterances.

In what follows, I attempt to force the archive to disgorge some of the words it has swallowed, even though the moment of speaking and recording has long since passed and time in the archive's belly may have

---

64   Carolyn, Hamilton *et al.* (eds.), *Refiguring the Archive*, Cape Town: David Philip, 2002.
65   Nick Shepherd, *The Mirror in the Ground: Archaeology, Photography and the Making of a Disciplinary Archive*, Jeppestown: Jonathan Ball, 2015, p. 76.

taken its toll on the recordings. The geographical location of these polyphonic, often fragmented echoes of colonial knowledge production speaks to the current discussion on ownership and to questions of restitution of cultural objects and artworks that were looted from African countries and taken to Europe during the colonial era. As with works of art from the African continent to which different meanings were assigned in European museums, historical sound recordings have often lost some of their resonance irretrievably in the archive.[66] Unlike works of art, recordings are very easy to restitute, at least as digital copies. But surprisingly, a systematic digital restitution that could also provide European archives with information about the significance of sound recordings – beyond their function as examples of languages or music – has yet to take place. This is also unfavourable for European sound archives, because historical recordings which remain interred exclusively in European archives are caged birds: they refuse to speak. At the same time, it is significant for our understanding of coloniality that historical sound recordings, apart from carrying spoken or sung text, allow us to listen in (belatedly) on a moment of colonial knowledge production. This makes them indispensable documents also of and for European colonial history. In other words: listening to Petrus Goliath, who speaks of the suffocating experience of having life casts made of him, may allow Germans to hear what most Namibians have known all along; it allows them to know their colonial past in different ways.[67] In some cases, as will be discussed in chapter 4, recordings may even contain commentaries on colonial practices of acquiring objects, on practices of stealing and abduction that have been called "collecting" for too long.[68] This means that historical sound recordings should be restituted *and* kept, which can easily be done in the digital age, because they speak to colonial knowledge production as much as to local and trans-local histories.

In the context of historical sound recordings, the notion of coloniality[69] highlights the permanence and troubling durability of epistemic

66 Felwine Sarr and Bénédicte Savoy, *Zurückgeben: Über die Restitution Afrikanischer Kulturgüter*, Berlin: Matthes and Seitz, 2019, p. 75.
67 See Hoffmann, "Widerspenstige Stimmen/Unruly Voices".
68 Linda Tuhiwai Smith, *Decolonizing Methodologies: Research and Indigenous People*, London: Zed Books, 1999.
69 Aníbal Quijano, "The Coloniality of Power, Eurocentrism, and Latin America", *Nepantla* 1 (3), 2000.

practices, which continue to operate in the archival legacies of colonial knowledge production. Symptoms of coloniality can be heard in recordings of speech and song with speakers and singers who were mostly referred to as *native informants* as much as their traces can be read in written documents of the colonial archives, and seen in historical and contemporary visual documents.[70] Yet different media, other genres of enunciation, as well as the material nature of documents, alter modes of receiving and understanding what is available as sources of colonial history, the forms in which histories are or have been represented, as well as what can be known of the assumptions and practices of the researchers and the policies of archives.

What can be heard, versus seen and read, is often not the same, even in relation to the same project of knowledge production. For example, an expedition can be interpreted very differently on the basis of its photographic, written and – as in the case of the collection assembled by the Austrian anthropologist Rudolf Pöch – cinematographic recordings, the anthropologist's diaries, the objects amassed, or audio documents, which will be discussed in the next chapters of this book. In what follows, I focus on one specific collection: the sound documents recorded by Rudolf Pöch in the Kalahari in 1908. Engaging with this specific acoustic collection and reconnecting it to photographs, objects, and to what can be known of the practices of the expedition during which the recordings were produced, I attempt to show how historical sound recordings speak as specific historical traces, and how they can also shift and expand contemporary understandings of the epistemic practices, their specific forms of violence, but also how we understand the positions of speakers, and moments or aspects of colonial history.

The swallowing, the suffocation, the misplacement or the outright loss of the acoustically preserved, often performatively and prosodically mediated meaning, of spoken and sung words, is not accidental. Therefore, the second chapter of this book will explore how a spoken text that

70   See Stoler, *Along the Archival Grain*; Elizabeth Edwards, *Raw Histories: Photographs, Anthropology and Museums*, Oxford: Oxford University Press, 2001. On native informants, see Mosa Phadi and Nomancotsho Pakade, "The Native Informant Speaks Back to the Offer of Friendship in White Academia", Shannon Walsh & Jon Soske (eds.), *Ties that Bind: Race and the Politics of Friendship in South Africa*, Johannesburg: Wits University Press, 2016.

was recorded in August 1908 in what was then British Bechuanaland was lost, and what practices, decisions and constellations of power led first to its disappearance, and then to the subsequent circulation of the cinematically captured scene of speaking. The starting point for the search for the lost spoken text of the speaker is the video clip *Buschmann spricht in den Phonographen* ("Bushman speaks into the Phonograph"), which has been circulating on the internet for years. The chapter begins with my reading of the short film created in 1984 by Dietrich Schüller, based on a cinematographic recording that Rudolf Pöch produced in the Kalahari in August 1908, and a recording with a speaker he called Kubi. Schüller's film silences this speaker for a second time. In order to understand more about the recording situation, the chapter follows Rudolf Pöch's journey through a border zone in the Kalahari. Further objects of analysis discussed in this chapter are audio recordings with two speakers whose names are documented as Kubi and |Xosi Tshai. These recordings were newly translated by Job Morris. In addition, the chapter reads example sentences from the same collection together with language examples in Naro, which were transcribed by the linguist Dorothea Bleek. The available documents give the impression of a context where people spoke under constraint, where Pöch was able to use the predicament of a severe drought and the crisis of the colonial war unscrupulously, to coerce people to undergo anthropometric study.

The third chapter discusses the retrieval of a speech act lost in the written index of the *Phonogrammarchiv* in Vienna. The recording in question is an acoustic document of the voice of Rudolf Pöch, who can be heard on the CD published in 2003 by the Vienna *Phonogrammarchiv*, which nevertheless does not index this recording accurately. Instead, in the booklet accompanying the CD, the recording of the anthropologist's voice was was listed as a recordings of "Bushman speech". This recording on which Pöch can be heard shatters his claim of linguistic competence and draws attention to the communication situation between him, his assistants, and the people he sought to study. In addition, the fear of |Kxara the Younger, who was employed by Pöch, surfaces as a topic in the recording of the anthropologist. He addressed the Naro speakers' fear of the anthropologist. These two recordings contradict the notion that sound recording is a harmless practice and reconnect it to the violent colonial politics which facilitated Pöch's expedition during wartime.

The fourth chapter examines two recordings, also newly translated by Job Morris, which disprove Pöch's claim that despite the fact that he robbed graves, shipped human remains to Austria, measured the bodies of people he met, and despite his massive acquisition or looting of the utensils, tools and weapons of the people he categorized as *Bushmen*, disagreements with those recorded did not occur. One of the recordings directly contradicts this myth: to my knowledge, it is the only known audio recording to date that explicitly criticises the ethnological appropriation of objects.[71] Thus, the last of the recordings discussed in this book leads back to the present, into the quiet repository of the *Weltmuseum* in Vienna. It also leads to the question of where else one might look when researching the provenance of objects of colonial appropriation, in search of alternative sources to the documentation of those who brought these objects to Europe.

71   A glossary of click sounds written with special characters can be found on page 153.

2 SPOKEN WORDS DISAPPEAR, A SPEAKER BECOMES A DANCER

> *[Colonial histories] can be made unavailable, unusable,*
> *safely removed from the domain of current conceivable*
> *human relations, with their moorings cut from specific*
> *persons, time, and place. They are histories that can be*
> *disabled and deadened to reflective life, shorn of the capacity*
> *to make connections.*

Ann Laura Stoler[72]

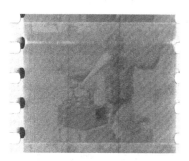 

Figs. 2 and 3: "Kubi" speaks into the photograph while being filmed by Rudolf Pöch, British Bechuanaland, 1908.

The speaker's name is given as Kubi, which may or may not have been his proper name. His image in black and white flickers on a grainy cinematographic recording, which was reworked as a film clip at the *Phonogrammarchiv* in Vienna in 1984, where it was also retrospectively synchronized with the noisy sound of the broken record ♪ Ph 789. Circulated with the title *"Buschmann spricht in den Phonographen"* ("Bushman Speaks into the Phonograph"), the clip shows the speaker's silhouette with dancing

72   Ann Laura Stoler, "Colonial Aphasia: Race and Disabled History in France", *Public Culture* 23 (1), 2011, p. 122.

arms, gesticulating. His words remain unintelligible. By means of ethnographic film, Kubi has become one of the "faint ghosts" of the colonial archive[73] which were produced during the tribal phase of European anthropology.[74] Kubi could be known as a narrator. He was one of two speakers who developed four variations on a theme in response to Rudolf Pöch's inquiries about the hydrogeological past of the area in the Kalahari where the speakers lived, together with other foragers, during August 1908. Perhaps addressing the visitor, most likely in conversation with each other, Kubi and |Xosi Tshai developed their take on the drastic environmental and social change they had experienced in the form of dialogic narratives. From what we can read in Pöch's sketchy documentation, and from what Job Morris was able to hear of |Xosi Tshai' s spoken text in recording ⅋Ph 786, their narratives addressed the deterioration of the environment and drastic changes of their way of life as a result of the colonial seizure of the land. Pöch recorded three of the versions acoustically. He did not bother to write down the first version he heard (although his notebooks show that he was able to write shorthand).

Kubi did not enter the public sphere as a narrator; nor is he known (in the present) as an expert on the history of environmental changes in the Kalahari from the late 19th century onwards. Despite being recorded several times, he is not known by his echo in the archive. Instead, his blurred image can be viewed in a film clip on YouTube, and frequently is. It is also accessible online on the website of the *Österreichische Mediathek* with the German title *Buschmann spricht in den Phonographen* (03:36 minutes). The cinematographic recording shows him speaking into the horn of a phonograph. In the film, Kubi's face is partially eclipsed by the apparatus; it is not clear whether the speaker or the technical device play the leading

---

73 Spivak, *A Critique of Postcolonial Reason*, 1999. Spivak writes of the Rani of Simur: "I should have liked to establish a transferential relationship with the Rani of Simur. I pray instead to be haunted by her slight ghost", p. 206.

74 On the appearance, or disappearance, of the historical figure of the subaltern, see for instance: Chatterjee, "After Subaltern Studies"; Premesh Lalu, "Sara's Suicide: History and the Representational Limit", *Kronos* 26, 2000; Lalu, *The Deaths of Hintsa*; Rosalind Morris, "Introduction"; Gyanendra Pandey "Voices from the Edge: The Struggle to Write Subaltern Histories" Vinayak Chaturvedi (ed.), *Mapping Subaltern Studies and the Postcolonial*, London: Verso, 2012; Prakash, "The Impossibility of Subaltern History"; Gayatri C. Spivak, "The Rani of Simur: An Essay in Reading the Archives", *History and Theory* 24 (3), 1985.

role. What is obvious is that both became actors in the heroic tale that stages Pöch as a pioneer of media-anthropology, a legend the anthropologist spun himself, and which was upheld in Vienna until the 2000s. The cinematographic perspective that Pöch chose for the recording on which the short film is based does not display any interest in bringing the speaker's face into the picture. The sound quality of the recording does not allow even Ts'aokhoe speakers to make out words in their own language. In the documentation from the first audio recording with Kubi, dated August 22, 1908, Rudolf Pöch writes:[75]

Kubi, unter den Anwesenden der älteste Mann, und ein guter Erzähler, wiederholt seine Schilderung der Elephantenherden, welche früher bei der Pfanne seines Feldes gewohnt haben.
[...]
Kubi erzählt sehr lebhaft unter fortwährendem Mienenspiel und Handbewegungen. Er sagt, die Pfannen seien früher voll Wasser gewesen das ganze Jahr, und hätten sich immer wieder gefüllt.
Kubi, the oldest man among those present and a good storyteller, repeats his description of the herds of elephants that used to live near the pan in his veld.
[...]
Kubi speaks very vividly, with constantly expressive face and hand movements. He says that the pans used to be full of water all year round and that they filled up again and again.

The short film *Buschmann spricht in den Phonographen*, produced by Dietrich Schüller together with Siegfried Hermann, Gabriele Weiß, and Karin Manafi in 1984, is based on Pöch's silent film of 1908. According to the film historian Wolfgang Fuhrmann, the clip has become one of the most frequently cited examples of early ethnographic film.[76] In the phonographic recording from 1908, which was added to the short film as an

75 Apart from the two recordings discussed here, Kubi is also listed as one of the singers and speakers for the wax cylinder recordings on the CD *Rudolf Pöch's Kalahari Recordings* of 2003 (tracks 5, 6, 11 on CD 2). The recordings were later transferred from cylinders to records in the archives in Vienna. Their contents are not documented in writing.
76 Wolfgang Fuhrmann, "Ethnographic Films from Prisoner-of-War Camps and the Aesthetics of Early Cinema", Reinhard Johler, Christian Marchetti and Moniqua Scheer (ed.), *Doing Anthropology in Wartime and War Zones: World War I and the Cultural Sciences in Europe*, Bielefeld: Transcript 2010, p. 338.

audio track, Kubi's words are drowned out by the noise of the recording device and the crackling of a broken record. No attempt was made in 1984 to include the words uttered by the speaker.[77] The film clip contains no subtitles, nor any other information about what was spoken into the phonograph's funnel. A series of selections and decisions have shaped this archival object. Beginning in the Kalahari in 1908 and continuing in Vienna almost 80 years later, the speaker's body and his gestures have been placed centre stage: because the spoken text was deemed irrelevant, the speaker's arms flutter meaninglessly on the screen. In the absence of words, the act of speaking resembles cinematographed scenes of pantomime or dance. David Chidester describes the colonists' practices of observing people at the Cape in the 17th and 18th century as a strategic response to their own apparent inability to learn local languages. At the same time, speech had been discarded as "unintelligible jargon that defied interpretation".[78] Perhaps cinematographic recordings of dance were popular in colonial ethnographic film for similar reasons: the people who were studied could be reduced to bodies by European anthropologists, and their utterances did not confront viewers with languages they were not prepared to listen to or make the effort to understand.[79] About a quarter of Pöch's film footage seems to be devoted to dance. Because of Pöch's choice to use a broken record for the filming of the scene, the very practice of cinematographic recording transformed Kubi into a dancer, and this is how his image entered the public sphere.[80] In the film, the distorted echo of Kubi's voice,

77 Britta Lange, *Die Wiener Forschungen an Kriegsgefangenen*; Assenka Oksiloff, *Picturing the Primitive: Visual Culture, Ethnography and Early German Cinema*, New York: Palgrave MacMillan 2001.

78 David Chidester, "Mutilating Meaning: European Interpretations of Khoisan Languages of the Body", Pippa Skotnes (ed.) *Miscast: Negotiating the Presence of the Bushmen*, Cape Town: University of Cape Town Press, 1996, p. 25.

79 Ts'aokhoe is described as a dialect of Naro (http://multitree.org/codes/nhr-tsa, accessed November 2018. Naro is a dialect cluster spoken by about 20,000 speakers in Namibia and Botswana.

80 Notes on recording dance appear in Pöch's notebook no. 12: pp. 1132–1134. On dance in early ethnographic film, see Valerie Weinstein, "Archiving the Ephemeral: Dance in Ethnographic Films from the Hamburg South Seas Expedition 1908–1910", *Seminar* 46 (3), 2010; on dance and in relation to the focus on looking at bodies and body language in people classified as *Bushmen*, see David Chidester, "Mutilating Meaning: European Interpretations of Khoisan Languages of the Body", Pippa Skotnes (ed.), *Miscast: Negotiating the Presence of the Bushmen*, Cape Town: University of Cape Town Press, 1996, p. 24.

juxtaposed with the rumbling of the phonograph and the sounds of a damaged wax cylinder amalgamate into an obscure, orchestrated sonic otherness. This is not as exceptional as it may sound. Rather, it is the audible paradox of many historical recordings, that demonstrates how colonial knowledge production deleted the recorded, spoken words of people who were perceived and phonographed as "natives".

As a result of a process of selections by the anthropologist, the archive, and subsequently the producers of the film clip, this particularly poor recording (Ph 789), conserved on a broken record, reached a wider audience than the rest of the 33 historical speech recordings from the Kalahari that are held in the collection of the Vienna *Phonogrammarchiv* and were already digitized and released on CD in 2003.[81] In the 1984 film, the noisy record adds ambient sound to the spectacle. This conglomeration repeats the celebration of (then) new technologies; the film conveys textual content only with the title that turns Kubi into a *Bushman*, as well in the opening and closing credits, in which he does not appear as a co-producer of the record. Sans subtitles, the elaborate synchronization of the historical sound recording with the silent film recording produced in 1984 has created a technical gimmick that repeats Rudolf Pöch's decisions: the visual as well as technical achievement of cinematography take centre stage.[82] As a result, the racialized figure of the *Bushman* has flickered across thousands of screens in recent years, with more than 10,000 views on YouTube.

This chapter traces the loss of narratives, which Pöch's sound recording and written documentation could have conserved if he had chosen to listen to the speakers rather than depicting them as savages. As mentioned in chapter one, speakers often used the situation of acoustic recording to communicate what was on their minds; many speakers also tapped into their repertoire of orally transmitted texts to perform these for the recording. As a result, on many historical sound recordings, two culturally specific methods of preservation meet: on the one hand, that of narratives or songs, which, through their genre-specific forms as his-

81   On voids in historical sound recordings see also Niklas Zimmer, "Percival Kirby's Wax Cylinders: Elegy On Archiving a Deaf Spot", *Social Dynamics* 41 (1), 2015: *Special Section Listening to Sound Archives.*

82   Britta Lange, *Die Wiener Forschungen an Kriegsgefangenen 1915–1918: Anthropologische und ethnographische Verfahren im Lager*, Vienna: OAW Verlag 2013.

toriologies and by means of formalized practices of transmission, have made interpretations of history spatially and temporally portable and have thus conserved them.[83] On the other hand, linguistic, ethnological or musicological sound recordings have archived examples of languages and music as collectable objects, for example in the form of speech acts, narratives or songs recorded on wax cylinders or records, thus generating the archive for disciplines including comparative musicology and linguistics.[84]

The cinematographic recording of 1908 presents the visual and acoustic recording of a speech act as an object of knowledge and an archival item. According to Pöch's written documentation, the speaker who was recorded phonographically and cinematographically conveyed knowledge about the recent past in the form of a narrative that was part of an ongoing conversation and, probably, also part of an oral archive. A sentence translated by Job Morris in Botswana in 2018, to which I will return, did retrieve a fragment of Kubi's commentary on the situation of those who were subjected to Pöch's research. Yet his sentence does not feature in Pöch's documentation. It was lost in the process of archiving.

This trace of spoken words we were able to detect suggests that Kubi's narrative could have provided an entry point into a specific discursive domain, in which the dramatic changes in the world of foragers, in the area of Ghanzi, in the first decade of the last century, were discussed by those who experienced this loss. In what follows, I will focus on how this potential point of entry to a historical oral repertoire was swallowed as a result of a set of preferences, a range of practices of colonial knowledge production, which aimed to archive the ethnographic figure of the *Bushman* as an exclusively visual, mute object. I argue that this particular loss of spoken text is not simply the result of an early, unsophisticated recording technique: two sound recordings with the speaker seen in the film were acoustically preserved in 1908, subsequently translated into Afrikaans for Pöch by the Naro speakers |Xosi Tshai and |Kxara, and then summed up and written down by Pöch according to the requirements of the Vienna *Phonogrammarchiv*. Pöch also noted down a synopsis in German on

83   Hoffmann, "Verbale Riposte"; "Listening to Sound Archives"; "Kolonialität".
84   Cf. Brady, *A Spiral Way*; Stangl, *Ethnologie im Ohr*; Sterne, *The Audible Past*; Lange, "Archiv".

one of the institution's pre-printed protocol forms. The acoustically inferior of the two sound recordings was elaborately processed into a "talkie" together with the cinematographic recording in 1984, and digitized later on. All the sound recordings co-produced by Pöch with speakers in the Kalahari were published in 2003 as a CD, titled *Rudolf Pöch's Kalahari Recordings (1908)*, by the *Österreichische Akademie der Wissenschaften* (Austrian Academy of Sciences), with an accompanying booklet. The recordings with the speaker Pöch called Kubi are not merely very poor acoustically; this loss of textual meaning extends into the present. About the 1984 short film, which is available on YouTube and probably originates from the Austrian *Mediathek's* website, the *Mediathek* provides the following information:

> *Rudolf Pöch – Arzt, Anthropologe und Ethnograph – filmte 1908 den über 60 Jahre alten Buschmann Kubi, wie er in einen Phonographen spricht. Dieser erzählt vom Verhalten von Elefanten an den Wasserstellen, die früher das ganze Jahr voll Wasser gewesen seien. Die historischen Filmaufnahmen wurden 1984 mit Tonaufnahmen, die von Rudolf Pöch zur selben Zeit gemacht worden waren, versehen. Sprache: T's-aukhoe*
>
> In 1908, Rudolf Pöch – doctor, anthropologist and ethnographer – filmed Kubi, a bushman who was over 60 years old, speaking into a phonograph. He speaks about the behaviour of elephants at the water pan, which used to have water all year round. In 1984, the historical film footage was supplemented with sound recordings made by Rudolf Pöch at the same time. Language: T's-aukhoe. (Journal *Wissenschaftliche Filme*, Teilverzeichnis Ethnologie, Afrika; Jahr 1987).[85]

The information on the *Mediathek's* web page reduces the spoken text to a single sentence. Because this information is not included in the actual film, it has become supplementary, secondary information that depicts a situation of speaking, which, despite its added soundtrack, seems to do without the speaker's words. Because of this (more) recent decision, interested viewers have to search actively for information on the spoken content. On its way to YouTube, this supplement was lost. No words are left there.

---

85   https://www.mediathek.at/portaltreffer/atom/018AA725-2F8-021EC-00000484-0189A3E5/pool/BWEB/, accessed October 2018.

This chapter explores how spoken words disappeared although they were recorded, and why it did not matter to European observers what exactly Kubi and |Xosi Tshai had said and how they said it. By asking what can be known about the specific recording situation on August 22 and 23 1908, I try to unpack its archival trace more than a century later. Referring to "trace", I do not mean to invoke the romanticizing notion of fading remnants of the colonial past that do not permit systematic analysis, which has been criticized by Ann Laura Stoler.[86] Rather, I use existing archival fragments, together with glaring gaps, to engage with the systematics of colonial knowledge production. The objects Pöch had amassed on his trip to the Kalahari are scattered between five Viennese institutions: the *Phonogrammarchiv* (The Phonogram Archive of the Austrian Academy of Science), the *Naturhistorisches Museum* (Natural History Museum Vienna), the *Weltmuseum* (World Museum), the *Department für Evolutionäre Anthropologie* (Department of Evolutionary Anthropology at the University of Vienna), and the *Filmarchiv Austria* (Film Archive Austria). As mentioned in chapter 1, these objects have been divided according to disciplines. For a reading-of and listening-to Pöch's journey through a war zone, his practices of extracting knowledge and appropriating objects, as well as the echo of the speakers' encounters with the anthropologist, these archival traces are partially (and virtually) reassembled in this chapter.

In this context, at times the acoustic traces resound as a particularly resistant element of the "collection", resonating with Gyan Prakash's notion of "recalcitrant difference". The fragmented echoes of specific subaltern speaking positions that we found in these recordings disrupt Pöch's sonorous tale of colonial knowledge production with people whom he called *Bushmen*, pointing to systematic absences and bringing to the surface the epistemological practices that produced archival objects.[87] As a strategy for revitalization of these objects or, as the Berlin artist group *Artefakte*[88] has called it, the (re)activation of scattered, isolated archival objects in the present, the systematic reconnection of archival material that has been separated according to the logics of various disciplines is crucial. In what

86   Stoler, *Duress*, p. 5.
87   Prakash, "Subaltern Studies as Postcolonial Criticism", p. 1477; Hoffmann, "Verbale Riposte"; Hoffmann "Oh meine Schwester, mein Rücken brennt sehr, und ich bin machtlos!"; Hoffmann "Wie ein Hund in einem Fangeisen schreien".
88   http://artificialfacts.de/about, accessed October 2018.

follows, sound recordings, cinematographic recordings, Pöch's notebooks, the photographs he took during his Kalahari expedition, the objects he obtained, which subsequently became ethnographic objects, the reports to the *Kaiserliche Akademie der Wissenschaften* (Imperial Academy of Sciences) in Vienna, and the publications are read and heard together.[89]

In order to trace how a speaker was muted and presented as a mime, in seeking to make sense of what he might have said and to understand the historical weight of a fragmented spoken text drowned in the noise of the historical recording, I must take a detour: I follow the anthropologist's journey to particular places and reconstruct some of his views and intentions. Pöch's documentation delivers scarce information on the speakers with whom he worked. Yet their positionality needs to be understood better to hear their texts. The figure of the anthropologist does not occupy the centre of my search, nor will I present a coherent historical narrative of his journey. Instead, I relate the loss of spoken text to the lesser-known archival objects and listen, together with Job Morris, to the still-resonant, translatable echoes of spoken texts. This approach may appear cumbersome, yet it is necessary in order to follow the trail of sound archiving, in the course of which many words were lost or omitted.

89   Regina Sarreiter, "Activate Facts! Von sprechenden Tatsachen", Martina Griesser *et al.* (eds.), *Gegen den Stand der Dinge: Objekte in Museen und Ausstellungen*, Berlin: De Gruyter, 2016; Rodney Harrison, "Reassembling the Collection: Ethnographic Museums and Indigenous Agency"; Barbara Plankensteiner, "Auch hier gilt die Regel, Buschmanngut und Fremdgut auseinanderzuhalten: Rudolf Pöchs Südafrika-Sammlung und ihre wissenschaftliche Bearbeitung durch Walter Hirschberg", *Archiv für Völkerkunde* 59–60, 2009.

WHAT CAN AND CANNOT BE READ

*When the hand that holds the trowel is black, it is as though
holes dig themselves, and artefacts are removed, labelled, and
transported without human agency.*

Nick Shepherd[90]

The photograph from the collection of Pöch's Kalahari journey in the
Naturhistorisches Museum in Vienna (Fig. 4) has not been published until
now. It shows an ox wagon without oxen, somewhere in German Southwest Africa (now Namibia) or British Bechuanaland (now Botswana). It
also shows a child who may have been fetching water, and the anthropologist, whose altogether unmentioned buttocks are sitting on an equally
unmentioned cushion.

I bring up the backside of the anthropologist here because, unlike
the body shape, skin colour, height, the bone structure, the form of skulls,
of ears, the teeth and, notoriously, the buttocks and genitals of the people
he meticulously studied, it has never been a topic for discussion.[91] The
anthropologist's backside does not surface in Pöch's texts, nor was it of
interest in texts about him, his travels, or his achievements as a pioneer of
photography, film and phonography in anthropology. It does not feature,
apart from in this picture, in the 2000 photographs of this expedition that
can be found in the *Weltmuseum*, the *Naturhistorisches Museum* and the *Department für Evolutionäre Anthropologie* in Vienna. Neither is it relevant. Speaking
of the backside of the anthropologist, I seek to foreground what colonial
knowledge production does and does not mention, what it speaks of and
what it omits. This again brings up questions about whose bodies were

90   Shepherd, *The Mirror in the Ground*, p. 42.
91   Robert J. Gordon wrote of the obsessive interest in studying the genitalia of foragers in
     southern Africa: see "The Rise of the Bushman Penis: Germans, Genitalia and Geno-
     cide", *African Studies* 55 (1), 1998; see also Martin Legassick and Ciraj Rassool, *Skeletons
     in the Cupboard: South African Museums and the Trade in Human Remains 1907–1917*,
     Cape Town and Kimberley: The South African Museum, 2000, p. 11; Alan Barnard,
     Anthropology and the Bushmen, Oxford and New York: Berg 2007, p. 20; Chidester,
     "Mutilating Meaning", p. 28., Sophie Schasiepen, *Southern African Human Remains as
     Property: Physical Anthropology and the Production of Racial Capital in Austria*, Unpub-
     lished Ph.D Thesis, University of the Western Cape, 2021.

Fig. 4: Pöch on his wagon, with an unnamed child, Kalahari, 1908.

discussed and how; who was – or felt they were – entitled to speak about whose bodies; and what did or did not appear in photographs. The pillow, at any rate, together with the young servant, refer to some of the small and larger comforts that colonial power brought with it, about which Pöch's own representation, as well as later descriptions of his heroic, arduous journey through the Kalahari, have mostly remained silent.[92]

In Austria, the anthropologist Helga Maria Pacher presented a list of the human remains that Pöch had exhumed, bought, or that had been "donated" to him in southern Africa, which are still kept in Vienna. In the 1960s, Pacher still unequivocally described Pöch's journey to the Kalahari as an exceptional, heroic undertaking. She wrote that Pöch had travelled 2600 km with his entire assembly of field equipment (at least three cameras and hundreds of glass plates, two phonographs together with cylinders and records, material for plaster casts, measuring instruments, etc.) "by

92   Johann Szilvásy, Paul Spindler and Herbert Kritschler, "Rudolf Pöch: Arzt, Anthropologe und Ethnograph", *Annalen des Naturhistorischen Museums in Wien* 83, 1980; Legassick and Rassool, *Skeletons in the Cupboard*, p. 10; Katarina Matiasek, "A Mutual Space? Stereo Photography on Viennese Anthropological Expeditions (1905–1945)", Marianne Kleum and Ulrike Spring (eds.), *Expeditions as Experiments: Practising Observation and Documentation*, London: Palgrave Macmillan, 2016, p. 192; Rudolf Pöch, "Meine beiden Kalahari Reisen 1908 und 1909", *Zeitschrift für Erdkunde zu Berlin*, 1910.

ox wagon, on horseback, on camels and on foot".[93] Pöch mentioned the support of the colonial governments in German Southwest Africa and in British Bechuanaland, as well as the assistance he received from the German *Schutztruppe* (the German colonial troops in in German Southwest Africa) in his reports and the few articles he published on the topic. His unpublished notebooks, which have been digitized only recently, convey a far less heroic picture of his journey through southern Africa, a trip that was supported by a network of German military, police, and European settlers. The structure of colonial knowledge production, its selective archiving, together with the imperial formations in which it operated, have made it far easier to learn about Rudolf Pöch than about the speakers who were recorded, the people who were examined, those who fetched water for him, the three drivers of the wagon with 18 oxen which had generously been provided by governor Schuckmann for the journey from Windhoek to Oas, the translators, the cook and the assistants, without whom neither Pöch's journey nor his research would have been possible. The pillow in the photo and Pöch's entries in his diaries speak of selective representation, which can be summed up as ethnographic lore. Certain aspects of the researchers' journeys and undertakings do not feature in the narratives he presented to the *Kaiserliche Akademie der Wissenschaften* (Imperial Academy of Sciences) in Vienna, nor did they appear in academic publications.[94] In order to speak about these unmentioned aspects of an expeditionary journey, it is necessary to change the terms of engagement. Nick Shepherd has described this change as a fundamental shift in the way colonial knowledge production and epistemological practices are perceived. This shift is the precondition for seeing, hearing, or reading particular elements of colonial knowledge production as a practice; it is also the precondition for the discontinuation of the neutralization of its violence.[95]

93   Helga Maria Pacher, *Anthropologische Untersuchungen an den Skeletten der Rudolf Pöch'schen Buschmannsammlung, 1. Heft: Herkunft des Sammlungsgutes, Maßbefunde und Lichtbilder der Schädel*, Österreichische Akademie der Wissenschaften, Rudolf Pöchs Nachlass, Serie A: Physische Anthropologie, XII, Band, Graz, Wien and Köln: Böhlau, 1962, p. 2; see also Sophie Schasiepen, *Schreiben über Dr Rudolf Pöch's "Forschungsreisen": Postkoloniale Kritiken und die österreichische Rezeption einen k.u.k. Anthropologen. Eine kritische Diskursanalyse*, unpublished Diploma thesis, Academy of Fine Arts Vienna, 2013, p. 127.

94   Rudolf Pöch, "Berichte an die Akademie", *Anzeiger der Akademie der Wissenschaften*, XLV. Jahrgang, 1908, p. 124.

95   Shepherd, *The Mirror in the Ground*.

The historical normalization of the absence of informants and assistants, who often appear as racialized bodies, points to the asymmetrical distribution of power which cannot be reversed retrospectively.[96] What is available in the archive, in the case of the spoils Rudolf Pöch brought back to Vienna, results from these power relations and his particular research interests. In this context, the cushions and the assistants about whom little can be learned are symptoms of particular selections in the process of archiving, and Pöch's own representations of his journey. This omission of practices can be destabilized by means of attending to particular images and sound recordings, which enables a reading of the silences regarding the intersubjective character of relational knowledge production, which was always based on cooperation.[97]

The results of relational knowledge production that appear in the archive, embedded in texts, sound recordings, or objects, are now owned by institutions, for instance in Europe. This knowledge held by museums, private collections, and universities, which, for a long time, have stubbornly refused the restitution of objects and artworks to their countries of origin, was and is still mostly attributed to the collectors. However, as already mentioned, the so-called collectors have not "collected" sound recordings, but rather produced them *together* with the speakers and singers.

The specific knowledge referred to here was and is – for example by means of the title of the published CD, *Rudolf Pöch's Kalahari Recordings* – attributed solely to the person who operated the recording device. This historical process of appropriation is related to representing the speakers as "prop or prey" in the heroic tales on phonographing "natives".[98] It is thus one of the ways in which imperial power has durably watermarked the processes of co-creating acoustic collections.

96 On the position of the *native informant* see for instance Phadi and Pakade, "The Native Informant Speaks Back". On speaking differently about practices of grave robbery and other violent research practices, see Anette Hoffmann, "Skandalträchtig Drauflosreden: Vorschläge zur Entsachlichung des Sprechens von der Erbeutung von Körpern, Objekten, und von Praktiken der kolonialen Linguistik, in vier Stücken", *The Mouth: Critical Studies on Language, Culture and Society* 9, 2021.

97 Anette Hoffmann, "War and Grammar: Acoustic Recordings with African Prisoners of the First World War (1915-18)", Ana Deumert, Anne Storch and Nick Shepherd (eds.), *Colonial and Decolonial Linguistics: Knowledges and Epistemes*, London: Oxford University Press, 2020.

98 See Ursula K. Le Guin, *The Carrier Bag Theory of Fiction,* introduced by Donna Haraway, New Castle upon Tyne: Ignota, 2019.

From Pöch we learn Kubi's estimated age, his place of origin and the suitability as a speaker the anthropologist ascribed to him:

So ist auch der Phonographist in besonderem Grade von der zur Aufnahme herangezogenen Persönlichkeit abhängig, und die Wahl ist hier umso schwerer, als das betreffende Individuum eine ganze Menge bestimmter Eigenschaften in sich vereinigen muß [...]. Typisch für diese Verhältnisse waren meine Erfahrungen unter den Kalahari Buschmännern. Ein alter Mann, Kubi, konnte sehr interessante und historisch wertvolle Schilderungen liefern, da er die ganz anderen Verhältnisse dieses Wüstengebiets zur Zeit der letzten niederschlagreichen Periode noch aus eigener Erfahrung kannte, da noch Elephantenherden und Rhinozerosse an den Pfannen ihren Stand hatten, die heute nur gelegentlich von flüchtigen Antilopenherden durchschweift werden. Trotzdem figurieren seine historisch und linguistisch gleich wichtigen Sprachdokumente nur als Proben des musikalischen Gesamtcharakters der Buschmannsprache, da dieser Mann leider gar nicht imstande war, sich an einen einmal gesprochenen Text bei der Wiedergabe zu halten. Außerdem hatte er eine für den Apparat ungeeignete Stimme und sprach auch seine Schnalze – für den Phonographen wenigstens – viel zu wenig distinkt aus (Archivplatte Nr. 789).[99]

The person who does the phonographic recording is particularly dependent on the person he records, and the choice is all the more difficult here because the individual in question must combine several qualities [...]. My experiences among the Kalahari Bushmen were typical of these conditions. An old man, Kubi, was able to present interesting and historically significant descriptions: From his own experience he knew of completely different conditions in this arid area at the time of the last period of heavy rainfall, when herds of elephants and rhinoceroses still visited the pans, where today herds of antelope roam only occasionally. Nevertheless, his historically and linguistically relevant language documents figure only as samples of the overall musical character of the Bushman language, since this man was unfortunately incapable of sticking to a previously presented text when reproducing it. In addition, his voice was unsuitable for the apparatus and he also pronounced the clicks - at least for the phonograph - far too indistinctly (archive record no. 789).[100]

---

99   Rudolf Pöch, "Technik und Wert des Sammelns phonographischer Sprachproben auf Expeditionen", *45 Mitteilungen der Phonogrammarchivs-Kommission der kaiserlichen Akademie der Wissenschaften in Wien*, 1917, p. 12, parenthesis in the original.

100   Pöch, "Technik und Wert des Sammelns phonographischer Sprachproben auf Expeditionen", p. 12.

Pöch states that Kubi lived in the area between Kg'au tshàa and a pan that also appears with the name "Kubi" in Pöch's record. The anthropologist estimated that he was over 60 years old.[101] Apart from the sentences cited above, Pöch does not mention the speaker in any of his available notebooks – the notebooks which may have referred to the situation of recordings are missing.

Far more can be read about Rudolf Pöch (1870–1921), after whom a street was named in Vienna.[102] Considered the founder of anthropology in Austria, Pöch had established his reputation as an anthropologist via his travels to Papua and to southern Africa, yet it was particularly the large quantities of objects, film, photographs and sound recordings he had obtained on his travels that became the basis for his career in Vienna.[103] After his return from southern Africa, Pöch worked at the *Phonogrammarchiv* in Vienna, where he archived the sound recordings he had produced with people in Papua, South West Africa and British Bechuanaland. In 1919 he was appointed the first professor of anthropology at the University of Vienna.[104] It was not until the publication by the South African historians Ciraj Rassool and Martin Legassick, *Skeletons in the Cupboard* (2000) appeared, that Pöch also became known in Europe as an unscrupulous grave robber.[105]

---

101   Protocol form for recording Ph 789.
102   The Pöchgasse is located in the 14th district of Vienna. See also https://monuments. univie.ac.at/index.php?title=Denkmal_Rudolf_P%C3%B6ch, accessed October 2018.
103   Schasiepen, *Southern African Human Remains as Property*.
104   Pöch, "Berichte an die Akademie", 1908; and "Berichte an die Akademie", *Anzeiger der Akademie der Wissenschaften, XLVI Jahrgang,* 1909; Pöch, "Meine beiden Kalahari Reisen 1908 und 1909"; "Reisen im Innern Südafrikas zum Studium der Buschmänner in den Jahren 1907 bis 1909", Sitzung vom 19 Februar 1910, *Zeitschrift für Ethnologie* 42 (2), 1910; Pöch "Technik und Wert des Sammelns"; Gerda Lechleitner, "Pöch, Rudolf", Österreichisches Musiklexikon online. https://www.musiklexikon.ac.at/ml/musik_P/ Poech_Rudolf.xml, last modified 2001; Schüller (ed.), *Rudolf Pöch's Kalahari Recordings*; Szilvásy, Spindler and Kritschler, "Rudolf Pöch"; Andrea Gschwendtner, "Frühe Wurzeln des Rassismus und Ideologie in der Anthropologie der Jahrhundertwende, am Beispiel des wissenschaftlichen Werkes des Anthropologen und Ethnographen Rudolf Pöch", Claudia Lepp and Barbara Danckwortt (eds.), *Von Grenzen und Ausgrenzung: Interdisziplinäre Beiträge zu den Themen Migration, Minderheiten und Fremdenfeindlichkeit,* Marburg: Schüren 1997; Susanne Ziegler, "Felix von Luschan als Walzensammler und Förderer des Berliner Phonogramm-Archivs", Peter Ruggendorfer and Hubert D. Szemethy (eds.), *Felix von Luschan (1854-1924): Leben und Wirken eines Universalgelehrten,* Vienna: Böhlau, 2009.
105   Legassick and Rassool, *Skeletons in the Cupboard*; Ciraj Rassool, "Restoring the Skeletons

The historical division of the collection according to disciplinary logics continues to neutralize the circumstances of the acquisition of the objects (see also chapter 4). The separation of objects by discipline has detached the cruelty of the desecration of corpses and the abduction of southern African people's remains from the violence of anthropometric photography, as well as from the presumed innocence of sound recordings. Yet the echo of Rudolf Pöch's dehumanizing research practices and his acquisition of human remains and objects, which should no longer be called "collecting", still reverberates in the recordings (see chapter 3). The human remains, which were most likely mainly of farm workers from southern Africa, held by the *Department für Evolutionäre Anthropologie* in Vienna, should no longer be called the "world's largest collection of *Bushman* remains", which retains the questionable, designation *"Bushman"*.[106] More than 110 years after the remains of the deceased were taken from southern Africa to Vienna, most are still unidentified and unburied.[107]

WHO IS "BUSHMAN"?

One of the detours that I must take before I engage with the recordings, which are the focus of my study is to discuss the term *"Bushman"*. This term is a historical exonym for people who were of interest to Rudolf Pöch. In the film *Buschmann spricht in den Phonographen*, the term *Bushman* appears as a stage name from the repertoire of ethnographic folklore.

Bushman as a term is a minefield: it is the result of chauvinistic, racializing, colonial settlement policies in southern Africa and parallel (at least in the 19th century) "racial research", related to murderous debates and practices of categorization, and a devaluation of ways of life, which ulti-

of Empire: Return, Reburial and Rehumanization", *Journal of Southern African Studies* 41 (3), 2015; Walther Sauer, "Die Geschichte von Klaas und Trooi Pienaar", *INDABA* 74 (12), 2012; Schasiepen, *Schreiben über Dr Rudolf Pöch's "Forschungsreisen"*.

106 Robert J. Gordon, "Gathering the Hunters: Bushmen in German (Colonial) Anthropology", Matti Bunzl and Glenn Penny (eds.), *Worldly Provincialism: German Anthropology in the Age of Empire,* Ann Arbor: University of Michigan Press, 2003. In Pacher's remarks it becomes clear that the human remains preserved at the *Department für Evolutionäre Anthropologie* at the University of Vienna are often skeletons of farm workers personally excavated by Pöch, remains whose "racial affiliation" is unclear even within the paradigms of Pöch's conception of race: see Pacher, *Anthropologische Untersuchungen*, p. 5.

107 Both Pöch himself, in his notebooks, and Pacher, in *Anthropological Untersuchungen*, give details of the locations of the excavations and in some cases give the names of the people whose bodies were excavated.

mately led to the expulsion and the genocide of those who had previously been categorized in this manner.[108] As a historical term, *Bushman* speaks to the categorization and hierarchization of the population in southern Africa and the colonial desire for control. As a colonially coined term, *Bushman* has an entangled and contradictory history, which, even in the sense of the concept of "race" from the 19th century, does not have a straightforward genealogy.[109] The German zoologist Hinrich Lichtenstein travelled in southern Africa in the first decade of the 1800s, some years after the increased resistance of foragers and local pastoralists to incoming *trekboers*[110] had been met with the establishment of *commandos*, in what was a concerted campaign to fight and kill foragers in the Cape interior and push the frontier of settlement further northwards.[111] Although many local foragers had been murdered by these commandos over the years, they were still feared by travellers like Lichtenstein.[112] To him the *Bushmen* were the aggressors at war against the settlers; they were resistant savages who refused to be forced into the colonial labour system, which exploited slaves and the local population.

The assertion of absolute, irreversible otherness, which perhaps only really emerged with the constructions of "race" in the 19th century, is summed up in Siegfried Passarge's phrase *"Bei den Buschmännern ist alles an-*

108 Mohamed Adhikari, *The Anatomy of a South African Genocide: The Extermination of the Cape San Peoples*, Cape Town: University of Cape Town Press, 2010; Robert J. Gordon, *The Bushman Myth: The Making of a Namibian Underclass*, Boulder, San Francisco and Oxford: Westview Press 1992; Robert J. Gordon, "Hiding in Full View: The 'Forgotten' Bushman Genocides of Namibia", *Genocide Studies and Prevention: An International Journal* 4 (1), 2009; Pippa Skotnes (ed.), *Claim to the Country: The Archive of Lucy Lloyd and Wilhelm Bleek*, Johannesburg: Jacana Publishers, 2007; Nigel Penn, *The Forgotten Frontier: Colonists and Khoisan on the Cape's Northern Frontier in the 18th Century*, Athens and Cape Town: Ohio University Press and Double Storey Books, 2005.

109 See Gordon, *The Bushman Myth*; Ute Dieckmann, *Hai||om in the Etosha Region*, Basel: Basler Afrika Bibliographien 2007; Mathias Guenther *et al.*, *The Bushmen of Southern Africa: A Foraging Society in Transition*, Cape Town: David Philip, 2000.

110 Semi-nomadic colonial pastoralists.

111 Nigel Penn describes commandos (both in their established official form as the so-called General Commando in 1774, and as *ad hoc* commandos, which were individually organized by *trekboers* at the frontier) as raiding parties led mostly by stock farmers, during which San were either killed or captured to be forced to work on farms: see *The Forgotten Frontier*, chapter 2.

112 Hinrich Lichtenstein, *Reisen im südlichen Africa in den Jahren 1803, 1804, 1805 und 1806, Zweiter Theil*, Berlin: 1812.

ders" (everything is different with the *Bushmen*).[113] What exactly was perceived as different by various observers over time and in various locations appears to have been by no means stable, and related to changing discursive uses and political objectives. Absolute difference was made out in their language, their history or the claimed lack thereof (while simultaneously referring to Darwinian classifications on an evolutionary timeline); it could be deduced from foragers' ways of life, from description of their bodies, or by referring to people's moral concepts and/or their relation to property. It referred to the social organization of various groups or people, who were lumped together under the name *Bushmen*.[114] Etymologically, the term can be traced back to the 17th century Dutch term *bosjesmann*. Particularly before the 19th century, *Bushman* seems to have described a way of life, which was never presented in an unprejudiced way. Francois le Vaillant, ornithologist and explorer, described *Bushmen* in his travelogue published in 1790 as:

> a promiscuous assemblage of mulattoes, negroes, mestizoes, of every species and sometimes of Hottentott and Bastards, who, all differing in color resemble each other in nothing but villainy [...] real land pirates who live under a chief without laws and without discipline, abandoned to the utmost misery and despair, base deserters who have no other subsistence but plundering and crime.[115]

Mary Louise Pratt, who has studied travelogues as particular genres of colonial narratives, speaks of distinct "narrative episodes" in which indigenous people of colour – not exclusively those referred to as *Bushmen* – were alternately represented as threatening *to* or menaced *by* settlers, explorers or colonial governments.[116] In the 1990s, Robert Gordon suggested using

113   Siegfried Passarge, *Die Buschmänner der Kalahari*, Berlin: Dietrich Reiner Verlag 1907, p. 17.

114   On early connections of language and concepts of race see for instance Bleek, *The Origin of Languages*; Shane Moran, *Representing Bushmen: South Africa and the Origin of Language*, Rochester, New York: University of Rochester Press 2009; Saul Dubow, *Scientific Racism in Modern South Africa*, Cambridge: The University of Cambridge Press, 1995.

115   Quoted from Ian Glen, "The Bushman in Early South African Literature", Skotnes (ed.), *Miscast*, p. 41.

116   Mary Louise Pratt, *Imperial Eyes: Travel Writing and Transculturation*, London and New York: Routledge 1992, p. 65; see also Paul S. Landau, "With Camera and Gun in Southern Africa: Inventing the Image of the Bushman, 1880 to 1935", Skotnes (ed.),

the term *Bushman* affirmatively, signifying resistance and social banditry.[117] Already in the 19th century, the term *Bushman* had been in use as a derogatory label and had experienced at least one moment of re-signifying by a heterogeneous group of people in South Africa's Drakensberg Mountains, who primarily survived by cattle raiding.[118] This group whose existence surfaces in the colonial archive had also created their own archive by means of rock paintings, a record which referred affirmatively to an definitively *Bushman* past and present.[119]

For the German-speaking researchers who subsequently travelled the Kalahari, the assertion of a fundamental otherness of bodies was often coupled with the idea that one could depict human evolutionary history on the basis of the people studied and depicted as *Bushmen*.[120] Pöch followed the physical-anthropological classification of his former teacher, the Berlin anthropologist Felix von Luschan, who had described "true Bushmen" with his list of 15 physical criteria in 1906.[121] In a breathtakingly circular argument, Pöch follows von Luschan's classification of *Bushmen* as a peculiarly ancient human race, discernible primarily by physical characteristics, and subsequently receives the enthusiastic approval of his teacher:

[D]ann möchte ich meinerseits erklären, dass ich mich den Ausführungen des Kollegen Pöch vollkommen anschließen kann. Es freut mich ganz besonders, dass er eine exakte Definition des Begriffs ,Buschmann' gegeben hat und dass er so mit mir die Stellung nimmt gegen die Reisenden usw. die in Südafrika und anderswo den Namen ,Buschmann' missbräuchlich auf allerhand Leute und Gruppen von Menschen anwenden, die im ,Busch' leben.

[A]dditionally, on my part, I would like to declare that I fully agree with what my colleague Pöch has said. I am particularly pleased that he has given an exact definition of the term "bushman" and that he thus takes a stand with me against the travellers etc. who in South Africa and elsewhere misuse the

Miscast, p. 129.

117 Gordon, *The Bushman Myth*, p. 7.

118 Paul S. Landau, *Popular Politics in the History of South Africa 1400-1948*, Cambridge and New York: Cambridge University Press 2010, p. 7.

119 Sam Challis, "Retribe and Resist: The Deliberate Ethnogenesis of a Creolised Raiding Band in Response to Colonization", Carolyn Hamilton and Nessa Leibhammer (eds.), *Tribing and Untribing the Archive*.

120 Rudolf Pöch's notebooks of his journey to the Kalahari, 1907-1909, numbers 1, 2, 7, 8, 9, 10, 11, 12, 13, 14, unpublished, *Naturhistorisches Museum*, no. 1, p. 100.

121 Felix von Luschan, "Pygmäen und Buschmänner", *Zeitschrift für Ethnologie* 46 (4), 1914, p. 155.

name "bushman" to refer to all kinds of people and groups of people who live in the "bush".[122]

To Pöch, the idea of a clearly definable and distinctive physique or race was the basis of distinguishing *Bushmen*, which he then depicted accordingly.[123] I use the term *Bushman/Bushmen* here to refer exclusively to Pöch's target group or objects of study, that is, as an always already predefined racial construction that came about during the particular episode of European history, which Achille Mbembe has called the "European tribal phase" of the 19th century.[124]

While I refer to the historical genealogy of the idea of *Bushman*, I would like to stress that this construction of a group had severe consequences for the people defined in this way: these kinds of historical construction were used to determine whose bodies, bones, images, objects, ways of life, and languages were of particular interest for research. Anthropological descriptions were also used to discuss which people could be used as labourers, that is, whom the colonial economy wanted to exploit, and who was seen as dispensable and therefore in danger of being expelled or murdered by military, police, and settlers. Travelling anthropologists, but also soldiers of the German *Schutztruppe*[125] who researched the population in the Kalahari, were involved in the practices of extracting knowledge from them, exhuming graves, shipping or selling human remains as well as looting the belongings of foragers which then became ethnographic objects. They also played an active role in the racist and racializing colonial economy that determined the value of the inhabitants of the colony as a labour force and as targets of research.[126]

122 Rudolf Pöch, "Die Stellung der Buschmannrasse unter den übrigen Menschenrassen", *Korrespondenzblatt der Deutschen Gesellschaft für Anthropologie, Ethnologie und Urgeschichte* 42, 1911.

123 Among the 2000 photographs held at the *Weltmuseum*, at the *Naturhistorisches Museum* and at the *Department für Evolutionäre Anthropologie*, many racializing, anthropometric photographs can be found. Some of them were used for teaching at the University of Vienna until the 1960s.

124 Achille Mbembe, *Kritik der schwarzen Vernunft*, Berlin: Suhrkamp 2014.

125 German colonial troops before World War I.

126 Dieckmann, *Hai‖om in the Etosha Region*, p. 79; Berengar von Zastrow, "Über die Buschleute", *Zeitschrift für Ethnologie* 46 (1), 1914; Franz Seiner and Peter Staudinger, "Beobachtungen und Messungen an Buschleuten", *Zeitschrift für Ethnologie* 44 (2), 1912, p. 283.

The problematic political impact of these colonial terms in the present is discussed, for example, in a recent anthology based on a South African research initiative on pre-colonial history. In one of its publications, the linguist Matthias Brenzinger argues for discarding the terms *San, Bushman* and *Khoi* as linguistic categories altogether:

> [T]here are no "San languages" spoken by hunter gatherers as opposed to Khoe(khoe) languages spoken by pastoral societies. Scholars such as Dorothea Bleek and Oswin Koehler saw themselves as "Bushman scholars" and because of this, they defined the languages they studied as Bushman languages.[127]

Brenzinger points out that there is no homogeneous, linguistically related group of San (*Bushman*) languages, but that this imagined unity (of San languages) always was and still is a mixture of economic, racial, and cultural criteria.[128] In her essay in the same volume, South African heritage scholar June Bam deploys the term *Khoisan* affirmatively as of identificatory use, but also as a strategic category and position in the context of recent demands for the repatriation of human remains and the restitution of formerly dispossessed land in South Africa by people identifying as Khoisan.[129] Bam is acutely aware of the historical construction of the term, yet she refers to a shared history of displacement, disempowerment and genocide that has been the result of this construction.[130]

127 Matthias Brenzinger, "Classifying Non-Bantu Click Languages", Lungisile Ntsebeza and Chris Saunders (eds.), *Papers from the Pre-Colonial Catalytic Project, Vol. 1*, Cape Town: University of Cape Town Press 2014, p. 87; see also Menán Du Plessis, "The Damaging Effects of Romantic Mythopoeia on Khoesan Linguistics", *Critical Arts* 28 (3), 2014, p. 574.

128 Brenzinger, "Classifying Non-Bantu Click Languages", p. 97.

129 Identification as Khoisan and thus as *First Nations* in the Cape can be a strategic move, in order to be able to put forward demands for land restitution and to recall and remind of a long history of persecution, dispossession, expulsion and murder. Examples of discursive formations in the present include positive identification as Khoisan as opposed to the apartheid term "coloured". For a recent discussion on the politics and history of subject positions, representational logics and knowledge formations around concepts of race, see Katharina Schramm, "Neue Technologien - alte Kategorien? Die Problematisierung von Rasse an der Schnittstelle von Wissenschaft und Politik", *Zeitschrift für Ethnologie* 139 (5), 2014.

130 June Bam, "Contemporary Khoisan Heritage Issues in South Africa: A Brief Historical Overview", Ntsebeza and Saunders (eds.) *Papers from the Pre-Colonial Catalytic Project,*

The implications of the ideas surrounding the term *Bushman* are evident in the assessments of researchers at the beginning of the 20th century: while they were of great interest to the German anthropologist Felix von Luschan, who therefore argued for their "protection" in a reserve, the geologist Siegfried Passarge suggested that the farmers and colonial officials had no choice but to kill them.[131] Pöch's attitude towards the people he studied seems to vacillate. On two consecutive pages of his notebook he writes: "we measure these primitive peoples by the yardstick of our ideals, which we delude ourselves into believing, yet which we do not heed ourselves".[132] Pöch then also mentions (his?) "racial hatred of the higher races for the lower races".[133] His last entry in the first notebook reads like a classic position of *salvage ethnography*, which at least makes clear who or what was threatening the survival of foragers in the Kalahari:

Darum ist es unsere Pflicht, Material zu sammeln von den ursprünglichen Rassen f. die Interessen der Zukunft. Heute ist die letzte Gelegenheit dazu, die wir fast unbenützt vorübergehen lassen. Wegen einiger Kokosbäume, wegen einiger Tausend Rinder schlachten wir ganze Urvölker hin.

Therefore, it is our duty to collect material from the original races for the future. Today is the last opportunity to do so, which we let pass almost unused. For the sake of a few coconut trees, or a few thousand cattle, we are slaughtering entire indigenous peoples.[134]

p. 123–133; June Bam, *Ausi Told Me: Why Cape Herstoriographies Matter*, Johannesburg: Fanele and Jacana Media, 2021; Adhikari, *The Anatomy of a South African Genocide*; Nigel Penn, "'Fated to Perish': The Destruction of the Cape San", Skotnes (ed.), *Miscast*.

131   Felix von Luschan, "Bericht über eine Reise in Südafrika", *Zeitschrift für Ethnologie* 38 (6), 1906, p. 895; Passarge, *Die Buschmänner der Kalahari*, p. 124.
132   Pöch, notebook no. 1, p. 99.
133   *Ibid.*, p. 100.
134   *Ibid.*

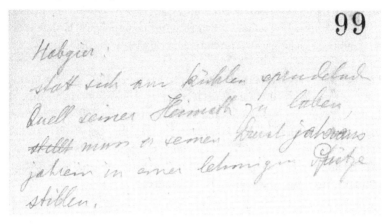

Fig. 5: Extract from Pöch's notebook no. 1, p. 99.

The material results of Pöch's journey through present-day Namibia, Botswana and South Africa include the human remains of approximately 171 people;[135] 2000 photographs, some of them anthropometric; film footage; 68 sound recordings on wax cylinders and records accompanied by written protocol forms; 1500 ethnographic objects; plaster casts and hair samples; notebooks (of which those from the period of the sound recordings are missing); as well as reports to the *Kaiserliche Akademie der Wissenschaften* (Imperial Academy of Sciences) in Vienna and a few other published articles. A systematic archival reconnection of this dispersed collection is still pending. In the intimate sphere of his notebooks, Pöch describes the impulse for assembling his extensive collection as greed (Fig. 5):[136]

135   This number includes individual bones, according to Pacher, *Anthropologische Untersuchungen*, 1962, and differs from the tally of full skeletons I gave in *Kolonialgeschichte hören: Das Echo gewaltsamer Wissensproduction in historischen Tondokumenten aus dem südlichen Afrika*, Wien: Mandelbaum, 2020.

136   The research project *Rudolf Pöch: A Scientific Pioneer*, funded by the *Fonds zur Förderung der wissenschaftlichen Forschung in Österreich* (FWF), which ran from 2005 to 2007 under the direction of Maria Teschler-Nicola (*Naturhistorisches Museum* in Vienna) in whose description Rudolf Pöch is once again celebrated as a media pioneer and explorer, aimed to bring together the collection's "unique and valuable archival holdings" in digital form. Unfortunately, this has not happened yet.

Habgier: statt sich am kühlen sprudelnden Quell seiner Heimath zu laben, ~~stillt~~ muss er seinen Durst jahraus jahrein in einer lehmigen Pfütze stillen.

Greed: instead of refreshing himself at the cool spring of his home, he must quench his thirst year in and year out in a loamy puddle.

Pöch's journey to southern Africa from December 1907 to November 1909 was funded by the *Kaiserliche Akademie der Wissenschaften* in Vienna.[137] In the *Zeitschrift für Ethnologie* (Journal of Ethnology, 1910), Pöch describes the goal of his journey, in accordance the study of the "last surviving remnants of the Bushman race".[138] Anticipating the rapid "disappearance" of the "Bushman race", which Felix von Luschan had postulated after his trip to South Africa two years earlier, he demanded:

1. *Möglichst eingehende Bekanntschaft mit Eingeborenen*
2. *Photo- und phonographische Aufnahmen*
3. *Gipsabformungen und Messungen möglichst vieler Leute aus verschiedenen Stämmen*
4. *Erwerb von ethnologischen Sammlungen, von Schädeln und Skeletten; Anknüpfung von Verbindungen mit dort lebenden Landsleuten.*

1. If possible, make close acquaintance with indigenous people
2. Photographic and phonographic recordings
3. Plaster casts and measurements of as many people as possible from different tribes
4. Acquisition of ethnological collections, skulls and skeletons; establishing connections with compatriots living there.[139]

Pöch followed von Luschan's recommendations regarding the desired "material" of study quite closely. This implied the desecration of graves, the large-scale anthropometric measurement and description of people's bodies, the systematic acquisition of objects, the production of plaster casts, photographs, cinematographic and phonographic recordings. Von Luschan, with whom Pöch had studied in Berlin in 1900/01 and with whom he competed specifically as a "collector", referred to foragers with the term "Überbleibsel" (remnants or residue) in his report on his trip

---

137   Pöch's trip to Papua, 1906, during which he assembled a similar collection, was self-financed.
138   Rudolf Pöch, "Reisen im Inneren Südafrikas", p. 357.
139   Von Luschan, "Bericht über eine Reise in Südafrika", p. 866.

to South Africa in 1905, thus portraying people as coming from another time.[140] In his report he describes travelling in southern Africa as less dangerous than 20 years earlier:

> *Damals Ochsenwagen, widerspenstige Träger, unbotmäßige Häuptlinge – heute ein dichtes Eisenbahnnetz und tadellose Schlaf- und Speisewagen, damals die Eingeborenen scheu und feindselig – heute zuvorkommend und mitteilsam, freilich ethnologisch nahe der Auflösung, aber gerade deshalb reif für die wissenschaftliche Einzeluntersuchung.*[141]

Back then: ox-drawn wagons, unruly porters, insubordinate chiefs. Today: a dense railway network and impeccable sleeping and dining cars. Back then: shy and hostile natives. Today: [they are] obliging and communicative, admittedly ethnologically close to disintegration, but precisely for this reason ripe for individual scientific investigation.[142]

Von Luschan's appraisal of the changes in the research situation from the perspective of researchers points to the process of colonization and successive disempowerment of the indigenous population in southern Africa, which would also create favourable conditions for Pöch's research in the following years. With regard to his itinerary, Pöch followed the assessments of Hans Schinz, who called for travelling to the Kalahari in order to study *Bushmen*.[143] He seems to have paid even closer attention to advice from the geographer Siegfried Passarge, who spent time in the Kalahari between 1897 and 1899, while working for the British Charterland Company. Passarge's book determines where the "real *Bushmen*" were to be found:

> *In der Kalahari wäre wohl das geeignetste Gebiet, um die Buschmänner zu studieren das Chanse- Kau-kau- und Hainafeld. Die Vorbedingung eines erfolgreichen Forschens ist aber die Erlernung der Hottentottensprache, die den Schlüssel zu dem Verständnis der Buschmannsprache bildet, zumal die Aikwesprache mit der Namasprache verwandt ist. Die Ergebnisse könnten von ungeheurer Tragweite sein.*

---

140 *Ibid.*, p. 895.
141 *Ibid.*, p. 865.
142 *Ibid.*, p. 865.
143 Quoted from Dieckmann, *Hai‖om in the Etosha Region*, p. 42; Dag Henrichsen, *Hans Schinz: Bruchstücke. Forschungsreisen in Deutsch-Südwestafrika*, Basel: Basler Afrika Bibliographien 2012.

In the Kalahari, the most suitable area to study the Bushmen would probably be the Chanse-, Kau-kau- and Haina-velds. The prerequisite for successful research, however, is learning the Hottentot language, which is the key to understanding the Bushman language, especially since the Aikwe language is related to the Nama language. The results could be of immense significance.[144]

Perhaps attracted by the prospect of conducting research with "immense significance", Pöch set out to study the people who were already defined as *Bushmen* in "the Chansefeld" (Ghanzi).

The catastrophe of dispossession, expulsion, imprisonment, and murder that people living as foragers experienced in the process of colonial settlement in the border region between South West Africa and British Bechuanaland surfaces in the historical descriptions of researchers and military personnel. A close reading of the spoken texts, which the linguist Dorothea Bleek[145] wrote down in this area allows me to read some of their experiences that appear as fragments in the linguist's transcriptions and translations. Unlike with audio recordings, it is not possible to revisit the acoustic echo of these speech acts.

Between 17 and 21 December, 1921, a speaker with the name Kukurib recalled several scenes of cinematographic recording, which in this way entered Dorothea Bleek's notebooks: "so many years ago, a white man came and photographed the people".[146] Kukurib listed particular film scenes, for which people danced, sang and made fire, and created beads. He also recalled a man with sandals, whom Pöch had filmed running up and down.

144   Passarge, *Die Buschmänner der Kalahari*, p. 134.
145   Dorothea Bleek (1873-1948) was the daughter of the philologist Wilhelm Bleek (1827-1875) who, together with his sister-in-law Lucy Lloyd, compiled an extensive written record of so-called *Bushman* languages, as well as stories, reports, and drawings of prisoners at Breakwater Prison in Cape Town, some of whom later lived in his house in Mowbray. The Bleek and Lloyd Archive can be viewed digitally at http://lloydbleekcollection. cs.uct.ac.za, accessed January 2021. See Andrew Bank, *Bushmen in a Victorian World: The Remarkable Story of the Bleek-Lloyd Collection of Bushman Folklore*, Cape Town: Double Storey Books, 2006; Wilhelm Heinrich Immanuel Bleek, *Über den Ursprung der Sprache*, Weimar: Böhlau, 1868; Dorothea F. Bleek, *The Naron: A Bushman Tribe of the Central Kalahari*, London: Cambridge University Press, 1928; Jill Weintroub, *Dorothea Bleek: A Life of Scholarship: A Biography*, Johannesburg: Wits University Press, 2016; Michael Wessels, *Bushman Letters: Interpreting |Xam Letters*, Johannesburg: Wits University Press, 2010.
146   http://lloydbleekcollection.cs.uct.ac.za/books/BC_151_A3_18/A3_18_0414.html, accessed January 2021.

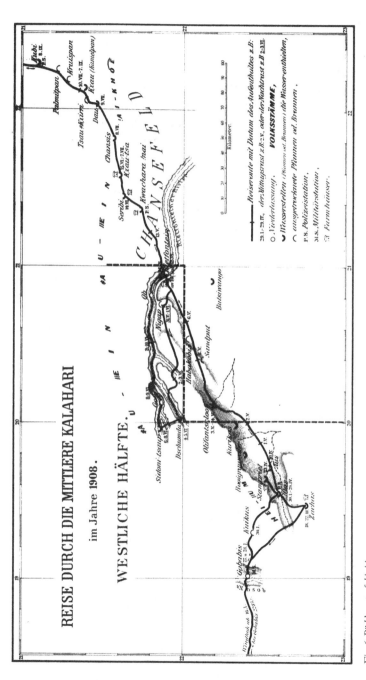

Fig. 6: Pöch's map of his itinerary.

In 2018 I was able to see these film scenes that were shot in Oas and on the farm Zachas, at the *Filmarchiv Austria*.[147]

Kukurib framed his narrative of Pöch's visit with an account of the severe drought, and he arguably tried to describe Pöch's apparatuses – the film camera as "a horn and a bag" and the phonograph "as an iron arm (…) that is winding" (A 18, p. 412). Perhaps Kukurib spoke faster than the linguist could write. What is clearly discernible from her notebooks is that Bleek did not make sense of the description of previous research that Kukurib shared with her, although she had followed Pöch to the Zachas farm in Omaheke, where Pöch had dug up graves with the support of the farmer Eduard Balzer – and where she may have done the same.[148] The pages in her notebook testify to Kukurib's insistent attempt to speak of research from the position of a person who was subjected to these practices. In Kukurib's reminiscences of his encounter with Pöch, the drought, policemen, as well as a Naron man who might have been | Kxara, feature. His narrative of observing the researchers culminated in sharing information about epistemic practices with others who experienced these practices:

A Bushman *[kweba]* it is, a man it is
with her parents he worked
when the Missis was small
ostriches, *korhaans*,
the eye, nose, ear, mouth
got clothes, no name
Bushmen *[kwe]* they are, three men they are
!Xam Kukummi [narratives] he did there …
(A 18, p. 423)

The list of words containing the terms "the eye, nose, ear, mouth" almost certainly refers to the recording of vocabulary in !Xam, which took place at Bleek's house in Mowbray in the second half of the 19th century. Kukurib thus shared his interpretation of a history of epistemic practices, yet Bleek

<hr>

147   The film scenes have not yet been digitized and some of them can only be viewed as negatives. The *Filmarchiv Austria* kindly allowed Margit Berner, Jannik Franzen and me to view the films in summer 2018. In Pöch's notebook no. 2, this list appears on p. 192.
148   Pacher, *Anthropologische Untersuchungen*, p. 5; Pöch, notebook no. 2, p. 133.

does not seem to have been interested in his understanding of the research on *Bushman* languages.

Until quite recently, the observation that many historical sound recordings were produced in the wake of war and in the aftermath of the systematic disempowerment of local populations was met with indignation and disbelief by archivists and curators of ethnological museums. In recent years, detailed provenance research on objects in ethnographic museums and on sound collections has confirmed systematic practices of looting and coercive knowledge production. The exponential increase of objects from South West Africa in German museums during and after the colonial war is particularly significant in this respect.[149] Many of these objects from Namibia, for example at the *Lindenmuseum* in Stuttgart, were delivered to the museums by *Schutztruppe* officers.[150]

My investigation into Pöch's practices of appropriation shows that his actions went beyond a "merely" parasitic relationship between anthropological practice and a colonial war. In fact, particular entries in his notebooks suggest that Pöch supported the genocidal war. As already mentioned, the anthropologist boarded in police and military stations in Oas, from 30 January to 29 April 1908, and in Rietfontein, from 1 May to 12 June 1908, he was escorted by the military and the police, he pitched his tent on white farmers' land, and relied on established relations between German *Schutztruppe* officers and white farmers.[151] Particularly helpful were Captain Kurt Streitwolf and Lieutenant Hans Kaufmann, who were both commissioned by the *Ethnologische Museum* to do research on the indigenous population and to send objects to Berlin.[152]

149 Gesa Grimme, "Annäherung an ein 'Schwieriges Erbe': Provenienzforschung im Linden-museum Stuttgart", Larissa Förster, Iris Edenheiser, Sarah Fründt and Heike Hartmann (eds.), *Provenienzforschung zu ethnografischen Sammlungen der Kolonialzeit: Positionen in der aktuellen Debatte,* electronic publication for the conference *Provenienzforschung zu ethnografischen Sammlungen der Kolonialzeit,* Munich, 7/8 April 2017; Paola Ivanov and Kristin Weber-Sinn, "Shared Research: on the need for cooperative provenance research using the example of the Tanzania projects at the Ethnological Museum Berlin", *ibid.*; Holger Stoecker, "Human Remains as Historical Sources for Namibian-German History: Results and Experiences from an Interdisciplinary Research Project", Geert Castryck, Silke Strickrodt and Katja Werthmann (eds.), *Sources and Methods for African History and Culture: Essays in Honour of Adam Jones,* Leipzig: Leipzig Universitätsverlag, 2016.
150 Gesa Grimme, "Provenienzforschung im Projekt 'Schwieriges Erbe': Zum Umgang mit kolonialzeitlichen Objekten in ethnologischen Museen", *Lindenmuseum* Stuttgart, 2018.
151 Pöch, notebook no. 2, p. 146.
152 Hans Kaufmann, "Die Aunin: Ein Beitrag zur Buschmannforschung", *Mitteilungen aus*

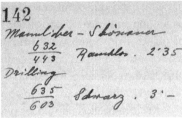

Fig. 7: From Pöch's notebook no. 2, pp. 140–142, entry from April 1908.

Pöch examined people on farms and at police and military stations.[153] He was able to use the so-called *native control registers* of the German colonial power, which listed the known African population (for instance in the vicinity of the police station), for his research.[154] Specifically the presence of the police and military allowed the anthropologist to coerce people to undergo examinations.[155] Pöch's boxes of human remains, plant and animal parts, photographic plates and objects were sent with the *Schutztruppe's* means of transport and on its transport routes. On February 8, 1908, while at the police station in Oas, Pöch noted that he had "received two bushmen for measurement". Most probably these two men were brought to him by policemen.[156] Pöch found graves (for example on the

den Deutschen Schutzgebieten 23, 1910.

153 Pöch, notebook no. 2, pp. 122, 124 and 130.
154 *Ibid.*, p. 128.
155 Pöch, "Berichte an die Akademie", 1908, p. 318; Pöch, "Berichte an die Akademie", 1909, p. 524.
156 Pöch, notebook no. 1, p. 67.

farm Zachas) with the help of white farmers who were able to force their farm workers to reveal their location.[157] His notebooks also testify to his active cooperation with the *Schutztruppe*. Pöch lists more than 3,000 rounds of ammunition, which he transported "from Oas",[158] probably to the military border station Rietfontein, in April 1908 (Fig. 7).

The catastrophe for the people who lived in Southwest Africa, the genocidal war, which also led to the eviction, dispossession and flight of the African population, features in passing in Pöch's notebooks. Mostly the war is mentioned as a potential obstruction to his work.

Am 5. März kam nach Oas die Meldung, daß die Hottentotten (Simon Copper) südlich von Aminuis in nördliche Richtung durchgebrochen seien, und daß infolgedessen auch der District Gobabis gefährdet sei [...] meine Arbeit erlitt jedoch keine Unterbrechung.

On 5 March, news came to Oas that the Hottentots (Simon Copper) had broken through south of Aminuis in a northerly direction, and that as a result the district of Gobabis was also endangered [...] my work, however, suffered no interruption.[159]

Pöch's attitude towards the colonized population as opponents of the German *Schutztruppe* appears in another entry on his notebook:

Eingeborene Stämme primitiver Rassen sind, weil sie keine ganz einheitlichen Organisationen bilden, viel schwerer zu besiegen, als höher kultivierte. Der eine fühlt den Tod des anderen wenig, jeder einzelne muss gedemütigt werden, es ist wie mit einer Schlange, deren einzelne Glieder sich noch krümmen.

Native tribes of primitive races, because they do not organize in larger communities, are much more difficult to defeat than more highly cultivated ones. One barely notes the death of the other, *each one must be offended individually*, it is like a snake whose individual limbs still writhe.[160]

---

157 Pöch, notebook no. 2, pp. 131–133. As Ciraj Rassool and Martin Legassick have shown in relation to the excavation of the bodies of Klaas and Trooi Pienaar, and as can also be seen in a photograph in the collection of the *Naturhistorisches Museum* and from his diaries, Pöch did not only exhume skeletons but also disinterred relatively recently buried bodies.

158 Pöch, notebook no. 2, pp. 140–142.

159 Pöch, "Berichte an die Akademie", p. 317; Pöch, notebook no. 1, p. 92; notebook no. 2, pp. 138 and 174.

160 Pöch, notebook no. 1, p. 96, my emphasis.

Together with the transport of ammunition, I read these sentences as an affirmation of the warfare against a population, which had already revealed its scope and cruelty in 1908.

HUNTING THE FORAGERS

While the persecution and disempowerment of groups identified as *Bushmen* by colonial settlers had begun far earlier in the Cape and the genocide of the !Xam speakers had already taken place there in the 19th century, according to ethnologist Mathias Guenther, Naro speakers in the area around Ghanzi were able to control the region they inhabited until the 1850s. In the second half of the 19th century, power constellations there again shifted to the disadvantage of foragers. With the arrival of Nama clans under Amraal Lambert in Gobabis in 1855, and even more with the successive settlement by white farmers in the 1890s, agricultural use of the land intensified massively in the relatively water-rich area.[161] Guenther assumes that the Naro speakers did not fight the settlement of white farms resolutely as they had done elsewhere, because they hoped that these could be allies in fighting off Batavana people from the neighbouring area to the east, who repeatedly attacked them.

I use the term "foragers" here to refer to people with a lifestyle of constant mobility and the practice of scouring not only the landscape, but also a more broadly defined, economically utilizable environment, for edible or useful things. |Kxara (the younger) and |Xosi Tshai may have been foragers in this broader sense of combing their environment in search of ways to secure their always precarious survival, in the process of which they acquired skills and strategies for survival in borderlands. This broader concept of foraging might include raiding and consuming the livestock of intruding settlers instead of hunting,[162] but it could also include contemporary modes of gathering of usable and edible things in urban environments. By widening the definition of foraging as a subsistence strategy, I challenge the understanding of it as a mythologized, Stone Age practice and suggest re-signifying it as a part of adaptation to the violent upheavals

---

161   Mathias Guenther, "From 'Lords of the Desert' to 'Rubbish People': The Colonial and Contemporary State of the Nharo of Botswana", Skotnes (ed.), *Miscast*, p. 228.
162   See Challis, "Retribe and Resist".

of the nearer colonial past. My understanding of foraging does not mark a specific point on an imaginary "developmental" or even evolutionary timeline, nor is it a practice which pre-dates sedentary life styles or practices of agriculture. Instead, it is a practice of subsistence that could and still can be used as a strategy of survival at any time.

The historical changes in the Ghanzi Ridge area can be described using Paul Landau's notion of "borderlands" as an area where struggles for supremacy and control took place during a certain period.[163] Borders in this sense need not be the current or former national borders, but rather frontiers of the areas actually subjected to colonial power.[164] Landau assumes that these periods of struggle for control were far less clear-cut than they have often been described to be.[165] Alliances between individuals and groups in this area were not necessarily organized around ethnic definitions, and certainly did not operate according to the definitions Pöch and von Luschan used to identify *Bushmen*. Moreover, diverse groups of mobile people in these areas had to adapt their ways of life to fluctuating, precarious and often perilous circumstances. On the (now) Namibian side of the colonial border, the violent history of their dispossession and displacement was one of the salient themes articulated in the language recordings Dorothea Bleek produced with Naro speakers or Hai||om between 1911 and 1921. Prompted to speak for the linguist's record, many of those who acted as informants mentioned the arrival of white settlers as a temporal marker of the beginning of upheaval and crisis. Some of the speakers mentioned their participation in big game hunting with white traders, and spoke of their work for white settlers.[166]

In particular, the foragers' loss of access to water and land due to colonial settlement of farmers, together with the decimation of game caused by hunting and the ivory trade, had led to the drastic dwindling of livelihoods for the foragers living in the Ghanzi area. In September 1908, that is, after Pöch had produced the sound recordings with Kubi, the an-

163 Landau, *Popular Politics*, p. 3.
164 For a discussion on frontiers, see Penn, *The Forgotten Frontier*.
165 Challis, "Retribe and Resist"; Carolyn Hamilton and Nessa Leibhammer, "Introduction", Carolyn Hamilton and Nessa Leibhammer (eds.), *Tribing and Untribing the Archive*.
166 On Bleek's research trips see Weintroub, *Dorothea Bleek*; and Andrew Bank, "Anthropology and Fieldwork Photography: Dorothea Bleek's Expedition to the Northern Cape and the Kalahari, July to December 1911", *Kronos* 32, 2006.

thropologist wrote in his notebook that the Swedish hunter Axel Erikson, together with the hunter Hendrik van Zyl, had shot elephants in the area in 1879.[167] What he did not mention – or perhaps did not know – is that van Zyl, according to Robert Gordon, had employed around "100 bushmen as shootboys".[168] A speaker from Grootfontein, whom Bleek refers to as Hai‖om (she writes Hei‖úm) and who appears in her notebook with the name Hataris, states the following in 1920:

> The Bushmen have no sheep, no goats, or cattle. Now they live only on *veld-kos*[169] and some work for white people. In her childhood her people hunted with guns, when she was tiny, they had bows and arrows. They bought the guns from Green, an Englishman with 6 wagons. He gave the people guns to shoot elephants and big game and give him the skins.[170]

The power relations within these hunting companies are difficult to reconstruct. However, Passarge's and Pöch's records show that even at the time of their travels, people who were labelled and treated as *Bushmen* were involved in expeditions and the colonial war as scouts or trackers. Passarge points out that *Bushmen* helped to supply water to the colonial troops at Rietfontein.[171] Pöch writes that "whoever understood how to use the help of the native Bushmen" could travel through the Kalahari without danger.[172] This suggests that the presence and support of foragers is clearly underrepresented in reports about the production of knowledge in the area, and that they played a crucial role with regard to the survival of many travellers. These comments also hint at mutual dependencies, and suggest that power relations were not as clear-cut as the travellers would present them later on. The involvement in big game hunting described by the speaker above also complicates the position of those who were called *Bushmen*, pointing to their active role in the transformation of this borderland. Yet how voluntary their involvement in these big game hunts was

167 Pöch, notebook no. 2, p. 174.
168 Gordon, *The Bushman Myth*, p. 192.
169 *Veldkos* refers to food growing in the wild, which was harvested by foragers.
170 Bleek's notebook http://lloydbleekcollection.cs.uct.ac.za/books/BC_151_A3_12/A3_12_050.html, on the first page the date "20.11.1920" is noted, and also the heading "Naron", accessed January 2021.
171 Passarge, *The Bushmen of the Kalahari*, pp. 18–20.
172 Pöch, notebook no. 12, p. 1122.

remains hard to assess. Landau describes processes of change in the *border-lands* that apply to Ghanzi for the second half of the 19th century: "wild-life dwindled, trade thrived, and customs were violated and removed."[173] Dorothea Bleek had met the Naro and Hai‖om she interviewed either on farms or in prison in Windhoek, where they were mostly serving time for cattle theft, were punished for their mobile lifestyle which had been criminalized by the colonial power as "vagrancy", or were imprisoned for attacks on farmers or police men. At the time of Pöch's trip, war and disempowerment were compounded by a prolonged drought in the western Kalahari, which forced those living as foragers either to stay in the immediate vicinity of functioning boreholes, for instance near police stations and farms, or to enter into working relationships with farmers. Kukurib recalls:

[we] found no ants, it is dry
it did not rain
rain does not fall, it is dry
I do not go, I am not going collecting, for at home I am
(…)
People go and pick resinkies [berries]
I do not eat them
Here I am
4 people went home, many people did not come
not water, rain fell
from the rocks we drank
The sun was burning, no water, rain fell on the stones
(…)
the sun is warm, the sun burns as we go fetch water
drink, bite, crunch
no water, it is dried up, water is dried up (…)
when the sun kills us (…)
(A 18, pp. 421-422)

The drought in the Kalahari during 1907 hampered his journey considerably, Pöch writes in his essay *"Reisen im Inneren Südafrikas zum Studium der Buschmänner in den Jahren 1907–9"* (Travels in the interior of South Africa to

173   Landau, *Popular Politics*, p. 3.

Fig. 8: Pöch's tent as a laboratory. Photograph without caption, 1908.

study Bushmen in the years 1907—9), published in the *Zeitschrift für Ethno-logie* in 1910. At the same time, he notes, the drought yielded the advantage "that Bushmen gathered in larger troops at the water holes".[174]

As in other situations, Pöch, like von Luschan before him, unscrupu-lously identified a crisis – in this case the drought, which coincided with the guerrilla warfare he mentions only sporadically – as a welcome oppor-tunity for his research.[175] In one of his "Reports to the Academy" sent by

174 Pöch, *"Reisen im Inneren Südafrikas"*, p. 358.
175 Andrew Zimmermann has pointed to Felix von Luschan's practices of exam-ining people and "acquiring" human remains. Von Luschan used the crimi-nalization of indigenous people by subjecting detainees to examination. At the Breakwater Prison he encountered "perhaps a greater number of Bushmen, Hottentotts and Griqua ... than had ever before been placed at the comfortable disposal of a scientific traveller" – see Felix von Luschan *"Bericht über eine im Sommer 1905 ausgeführte Reise in Südafrika"*, Bundesarchiv, Potsdam, cited in Andrew Zimmermann, "Adventures in the Skin Trade: German Anthropology and Colonial Corporeality", Penny and Bunzl (eds.), *Worldly Provincialism*, 2003, p. 163. During the colonial war and thereafter, von Luschan made contact with German military officials to acquire human remains from German South West Africa; see also Holger Stoecker, Thomas Schnalke and Andreas Winkelmann (eds.), *Sammeln, Erforschen, Zurückgeben? Menschliche Gebeine aus der Kolonialzeit in akademischen und musealen Sammlungen*, Berlin: Ch. Links Verlag, 2013; Holger Stoecker and Vilho Shigwedha, "Human Re-

Pöch during his trip to Vienna, he describes the settlers' control of the remaining water points, in this case a borehole: "The land around the pan is owned by the merchant Weatherilt".[176] The impact of the colonial seizure and privatization of land in the area created a severe crisis for foragers who lived in the area, because it meant loss of access to wells and water holes. Pöch writes that "the tent was pitched near the pan so that *Bushmen* fetching water could not easily be missed".[177] This sentence describes a hunting scene: Pöch lay in wait for people who did not have much choice but to fetch water at this place during the drought.[178] At this pan, Pöch writes, he was able to "once again apply the entire apparatus of modern anthropological research" to people who could not avoid him. Every individual in the group "who came to Kamelpan during the time I was there, excluding the children, was physically-anthropologically examined and photographed (83 people)".[179] If Pöch was able to coerce all adult individuals, without exception, to endure the procedures of anthropometric measurement, this means that they must have had little choice. In this case it was their need to access water that he exploited, while in Rietfontein Pöch had likely made use of foragers' dependency on the infrastructure provided by the police station, or otherwise the support of the military, to force people to undergo the procedure of examination. The situations Pöch describes show that the anthropologist did *not* study independent foragers. Rather, he imposed his presence on people who already lived under the ever-increasing constraints of colonization and whose survival was acutely threatened by war and drought. Most of the people he subjected to his studies lived in the vicinity of police stations, or on farms.

While Pöch states that people who lived near the Oas police station agreed to be measured and receive payment in food, in the vicinity of the Rietfontein military base, his collaboration with the *Schutztruppe* invested

---

mains in German Collections", *Human Remains and Violence* 4 (2), 2018.
176 Pöch, "Berichte an die Akademie" (1908), p. 522.
177 *Ibid.*
178 According to Marie Muschalek, hunting vocabulary was also commonly used to refer to patrols in search of potential labourers. See Marie Muschalek, *Violence as Usual: policing and the Colonial State in German Southwest Africa*, Ithaka and London: Cornell University Press, 2019, p. 138.
179 *Ibid.*, p. 524.

him with the power to summon foragers for his anthropometric studies[180] or to visit their dwelling places escorted by a specially assembled military camel patrol (Fig. 20).[181]

The fact that many of the people who were examined on farms were employed by white farmers appears in Pöch's notes on his activities on the farm Zachas, where he measured four farmworkers, including a woman named Rudolfine, whom he describes as a "Hereroweib (*Waschfrau*)".[182] In 1921, the linguist Dorothea Bleek went to study people on the same farm. This suggests that some farmers - like Eduard Balzer, the owner of Zachas (Bleek writes Tsaxas) - were known among the researchers for supporting their studies on humans.[183]

The precarious situation of the speakers needs to be taken into account when interpreting the acoustic recordings and their ambiguous content. Beyond a grammatical sense, the notion of "free speech" becomes doubtful in this respect. The fact that many of the speakers were measured and photographed before they spoke into the funnel, points to their precarious situation. It also means that, at least from Pöch's side, those who spoke had already been positioned as objects of investigation before they uttered a word into the phonograph.

Pöch amassed a considerable quantity of objects, produced botanical surveys, took stereo-photographs of landscapes and recorded speech samples for the *Phonogrammarchiv* in Vienna, yet his main interest was in the physical anthropology of the people he conceived of as "remnants" from an earlier evolutionary state of humanity. He notes that the anthropometric examinations took a total of six hours per person. To the people he examined, Pöch notes, he gifted a pound of rice, some salt, some sugar and tobacco in return.[184]

The staged ethnographic scene presented in the photograph, of the anthropologist's tent as a laboratory, shows the technical apparatus of recording: |Kxara (in the photograph, second from the left) whom

180   *Ibid.*, p. 262 and 434.
181   *Ibid.*, p. 435; Pöch, *"Meine beiden Kalahari Reisen 1908 und 1909"*, p. 24.
182   Pöch, notebook no. 2, p. 122.
183   Bleek refers to Tsaxas/Zachas twice: once on page 1 of her notebook no. 10 and once on page 19, where she speaks of Tsaxas and "some of Balzer's sort of bushmen". See http:// lloydbleekcollection.cs.uct.ac.za/books/BC_151_A3_10/index.html, accessed February 2022.
184   Pöch, "Berichte an die Akademie", 1908, p. 262.

Pöch calls his "cook and servant" and who also translated for him (see chapter 3) operated the phonograph, in front of which one person was sitting, while two other people were re-enacting anthropometric measurements. Another camera can be seen to the left of the tent in the photograph. The boxes in and around the tent indicate further equipment or objects already seized.

PRODUCING SOUND RECORDINGS IN KG'AU TSHÀA

That a white man is in Kxau [Kg'au tshàa], the people
know

Tsuǂnoa[185]

Fig. 9: Portrait of |Xosi Tshai, 1908.

185   Recording Ph 772, 13 August 1908, Kg'au tshàa.

Beyond the linguistic examples transcribed by Pöch, little can be read of the Naro speakers with whom Pöch was in contact. They were photographed, measured, and described; how they responded to or commented on these practices does not feature in Pöch's texts. In one of his reports to the *Akademie*, which Pöch sent to Vienna while still on his trip, he mentions interviewing older people:

> [...] *über Sitten, Gebräuche und über die Verhältnisse welche im Land herrschten, als die Betchuanen und noch früher, als die Hottentotten ins Land zu kommen pflegten. Unter meinen Gewährsmännern befand sich auch der frühere Diener S. Passarge's, Koschep (|Xosi). Dann ließ ich mir von alten Leuten von dem früheren Wildreichtum des Chansefeldes erzählen, das damals unter viel günstigeren Wasserverhältnissen auch Elephanten, Rhinozerosse und Giraffen beherbergte. Eine dieser Erzählungen, worin beschrieben wird, wie sich die Elephanten in dem Wasser und Schlamme von Kamelpan wälzten, ist phonographisch festgehalten (wie oben erwähnt, ist diese Pfanne nun ganz trocken [...]*

[...] about customs, traditions and the conditions that prevailed in the country when the *Bechuanen* and even earlier when the Hottentots used to come into the country. Among my informants was also S. Passarge's former servant, Koschep (|Xosi). Then I asked old people to tell me about the former abundance of game in the Chansefeld [Ghanzi], which at that time, under much more favourable water conditions, was also home to elephants, rhinoceroses and giraffes. One of these stories, which describes how the elephants rolled in the water and in the mud of *Kamelpan* is recorded phonographically (as mentioned above, this pan is now completely dry).[186]

Pöch's report, from which this extract is taken, was presented during the meeting of the *Kaiserliche Akademie der Wissenschaften* (Imperial Academy of Sciences) in Vienna on December 3, 1908. It documents Pöch's interest in environmental history, which probably prompted Kubi and |Xosi Tshai's account of past water conditions in the area. Furthermore, one of the speakers is introduced indirectly as Pöch's most important informant. Without any apparent irony, Pöch describes |Xosi Tshai as *Bushman* by profession in the protocol form for recording Ph 771; |Xosi Tshai had been in the service of travellers since he was ten years old.

---

186   *Ibid.*, p. 524.

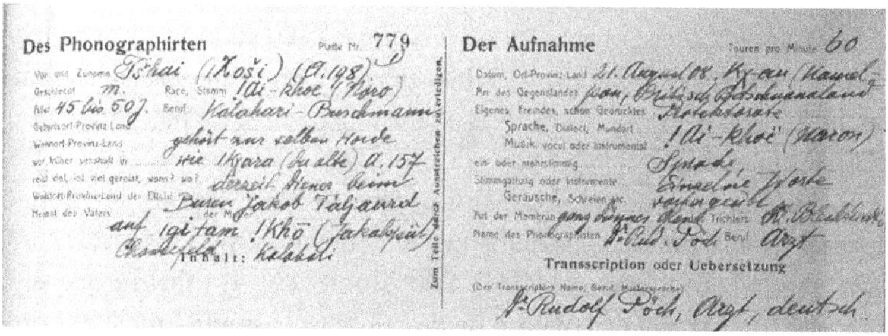

Des Phonographirten Platte Nr. 779

Vor- und Zuname: Tshai (|Koši) (A.198)

Geschlecht: m. Race, Stamm: |Ai-khoe (Naro)

Alter: 45 bis 50 J. Beruf: Kalahari-Buschmann

gehört zur selben Horde wie |Kara (der alte) A. 157

derzeit Diener beim Buren Jakob Taljaard

auf |gi farm !Khō (Jakalspütz)

Inhalt:

Zum Teile durch Ausstreichen zu erledigen.

Der Aufnahme Touren pro Minute: 60

Datum, Ort-Provinz-Land: 21. August 08

Sprache, Dialect, Mundart

Musik, vocal oder instrumental: !Ai-khoe (Naron)

ein- oder mehrstimmig: Sprache

Stimmgattung oder Instrumente: Einzelne Worte

Geräusche, Schreien etc.

Art der Membran; Trichter

Name des Phonographisten: Dr. Rud. Pöch Beruf: Arzt

Transscription oder Uebersetzung

Dr. Rudolf Pöch, Arzt, deutsch

Fig. 10: Extract from the protocol form for recording Ph 779, Phonogrammarchiv, Vienna.

As the figure of the professional *Bushman* – or the travelling informant – |Xosi Tshai's faint silhouette haunts the ethnographic literature about the area around Ghanzi and the *Bushmen* of the *Chansefeld* (Ghanzi). The Prussian geologist Siegfried Passarge called him his "faithful companion Koschep".[187] |Xosi Tshai read animal tracks for Passarge, and taught him to read the landscape and find his way around in the Kalahari. Most importantly,[188] |Xosi Tshai shared his understanding of the formation of the pan craters in the limestone karst of the Ghanzi Ridge with the geologist. |Xosi Tshai's knowledge was based on his long-term observation of the behaviour of large animals at the water holes.[189] He also spoke to Passarge about the history of Naro speakers in the Ghanzi area.[190] This documented process of relational knowledge production, during which |Xosi Tshai's observations of the modification of the landscape that was caused by the behaviour of large mammals was transmuted by Passarge into geological knowledge, which the geologist then presented in his book. In particular, |Xosi Tshai's information on the history of the Naro speakers which appears in Passarge's book, prompted the German anthropologist Gustav Fritsch to dismiss the latter as a "*Bushman* historian" and a liar in his review of Passarge's publications.[191] Most likely, Fritsch discredited |Xosi Tshai as belonging to a "tribe notorious for its mendacity" because his interpretation of his own community's history did not correspond with Fritsch's

187 Siegfried Passarge, *Die Kalahari: Versuch einer physisch-geographischen Darstellung der Sandfelder des südafrikanischen Beckens*, Berlin: Dietrich Reimer 1904, p. 324.

188 *Siegfried* Passarge, *Die Kalahari* p. 324.

189 *Ibid.*

190 *Ibid.*, p. 114.

191 Gustav Fritsch, "Die Buschmänner der Kalahari von S. Passarge", *Zeitschrift für Ethnologie* 38 (1/2), 1906, p. 73.

ideas about the social organization of *Bushmen*.[192] 90 years after the publication of Passarge's *The Kalahari*, |Xosi Tshai became a credible informant on the history of the Naro-speakers of the Ghanzi area for the ethnologist Mathias Guenther.[193]

Pöch did not meet |Xosi Tshai by chance: He mentions him in his notebooks in April 1908, months before arriving in the Ghanzi area to stay from July to September 1908. Pöch's notes suggest that he actively searched for |Xosi Tshai, whom he describes as Passarges' most important informant. He writes: "Buur Talliat in Quagga [sic] ... [illegible] *has* Passarges Bushman".[194] Again, the anthropologist's notes testify to his attitude towards the people he called *Bushmen*: in Pöch's notes, |Xosi Tshai appears to be owned by the farmer rather than employed by him. In the protocol for the voice recording he produced with the speaker for the *Phonogrammarchiv* in Vienna, Pöch describes |Xosi Tshai as *Ai-Khoe* or *Naron*. |Xosi Tshai articulated his name for the recording on 23 August 1908. According to Pöch, he begins recording Ph 787 with information about himself:

Ich bin |Xosi, ich bin Tshai (er hat nämlich 2 Namen).

Ich wohne auf Jackalspüt (– wörtl. Bedeutung des Buschmannnamens

|Gi Tam!Ko ist Tanzplatzpfanne)

Ich arbeite bei Jakob (Taljaard).

Der Doktor ruft,

Schnell bin ich da.

Jakob verlangt viel Geld.

Jedoch ich bekomme es nicht.

Es ist ein Jammer.

Ich bin |Xosi, ich bin Tshai.

Für Passarge habe ich gearbeitet.

Bei der Charterland Company.

Auf Chansis [Ghanzi] kamen wir zusammen.

Nach Kaukau gingen wir.

Nach /Gam gingen wir.

---

192   *Ibid.*, p. 72.
193   Mathias Guenther, "'Lords of the Desert Land': Politics and Resistance of the Ghanzi Basarwa of the 19th Century", *Botswana Notes and Records* 29, 1997, p. 123.
194   Pöch, notebook no. 2, p. 146, my translation.

I am |Xosi, I am Tshai (because he has 2 names).
I live at Jackalspüt (- lit. meaning of the Bushman's name
|Gi Tam!Ko is dance floor pan)
I work for Jakob (Taljaard).[195]
The doctor calls,
Quickly I am there.
Jakob demands a lot of money.
However, I do not get it.
It's a shame.
I am |Xosi, I am Tshai.
I worked for Passarge.
At Charterland Company.
On Chansis [Ghanzi] we came together.
To Kaukau we went.
To |Gam we went.
[Protocol form for recording Ph 787, brackets in original].

|Xosi Tshai inserted his name twice into the example sentences, perhaps seeking to prevent further distortion.[196] Nevertheless, he appears in Pöch's report to the Academy as "Koschep", which is the name with which Passarge had referred to him. His double name, which he pronounced for the recording, is written in brackets.[197] Before he met the Austrian anthropologist, |Xosi Tshai had already worked for the hunter Robertson, the farmer and cattle trader Franz Müller, as well as for the geologist Passarge and the farmer Taljaard.[198] According to Pöch, in the recordings cited above |Xosi Tshai related his experiences while being employed on colonial farms, which sounds like forced labour. Whether |Xosi Tshai hoped that the details he shared would travel remains unknown. He may have tried

195 A website on the history of Ghanzi presents the Taljaard family as among the first white settlers in the D'kar area: http://ghanzigesk.wixsite.com/ghanzi/a-short-history-of-ghanzi-district, accessed August 2019.
196 |Xosi Tshai is not the only speaker who has added an acoustic signature to his recording. Britta Lange describes how a speaker shouted his name into the funnel at the end of a recording, and thus signed his recording acoustically, see "Denken Sie selber über die Sache nach"; Abdulaye Niang, a prisoner of war from Senegal, wrote his name in Arabic script on the commission's recording sheet – see Hoffmann, *Knowing by Ear*.
197 Pöch, "Berichte an die Akademie", p. 524.
198 Protocol form for recording Ph 797.

to correct his name; he carefully articulated his value as an informant, and he spoke of the unfair treatment he expected from the farmer. The sense of *mésentente* and the suspension of communication is strong here: Pöch's main concerns were the insertion of words in Nama (Khoekhoegowab), which he was worried would compromise the object he sought to bring back to Vienna: linguistic specimens. The stated aim, after all, was "to study their languages and make linguistic-phonetic recordings for the *Phonogramarchiv* of the *Kaiserliche Akademie der Wissenschaften*". Perhaps |Xosi Tshai's accusation prompted Pöch to make the following statement:[199]

Zur Erkärung dieser Rede: Ich habe Tshai (|Xosi) dem Buren Jakob Taljaard für etwa eine Woche abgemietet. Der Bur machte sich die Situation zu nutze und begehrte zwei Pfund Entschädigung, obzwar weder Tshai (|Xosi) noch sein Ersatzmann einen Penny beziehen; es ärgert nun den Buschmann, dass er den weiten Weg von Jakalspüt nach Kamelpan u. zurück machen und sich plagen muss, während sein Herr, wie er richtig voraussieht, die zwei Pfund einstecken wird.

To explain this speech: I rented Tshai (|Xosi) from the Boer Jakob Taljaard for about a week. The Boer took advantage of the situation and demanded two pounds' compensation, although neither Tshai (|Xosi) nor his substitute receive a penny; it now annoys the Bushman that he has to make the long journey from Jakalsput to Kamelpan and back and toil, while his master, as he correctly foresees, will pocket the two pounds.[200]

Apparently the practice of exchanging black workers was common: in his report *Mitteilungen aus den deutschen Schutzgebieten*, about his exploration of the Omaheke from 1910 to 1912, Franz Seiner writes that a *Bushman* "named Sepp, who had been in the service of the farmer Deckert at Neufeld without interruption for twelve years" was rented out by "the farmer in return for a Herero for the next few months".[201] Pöch's assertion that the farmer Taljaard *had* |Xosi Tshai proved true in the sense that Pöch was able to hire |Xosi Tshai as an informant from the farmer. Pöch's notes show that he knew that |Xosi Tshai would not be paid for his service. Like other speakers in many other recording situations, |Xosi Tshai made use

---

199   Protocol form for recording Ph 787, Pöch, "Berichte an die Akademie", 1909, p. 437.
200   *Ibid.*
201   Franz Seiner, "Die Bastard Buschleute der Nord-Kalahari", *Mitteilungen aus den deutschen Schutzgebieten* 26 (3), 1913, p. 228.

of the opportunity to speak into the phonograph to air his assessment of his own situation (see chapter 1). Unfortunately, Job Morris was unable to retranslate his recordings because, despite recent sound editing, the quality of the recordings is very poor. The translations from the transcripts can thus not be verified. However, |Xosi Tshai's complaint appears to be a transcription, rather than a summary, from his sentences in Naro. Thus, a mediated statement on the practice of renting out workers from the point of view of a speaker who was subjected to this practice did enter the colonial archive. While his accounts on Naro history, which appeared in Passarge's text, did spark discussion and were picked up again by Guenther, |Xosi Tshai's spoken account has so far not been consulted as a source of colonial history. Yet it does offer a significantly different perspective from Seiner's and Pöch's comments on this practice of forced labour from which both of them benefitted. Because Job Morris could not retranslate the spoken text from the recording, Xosi Tshai's account can only be read through the filter of the transcription.

The transcriptions of various genres of recording appear quite differently in Pöch's protocol forms. Particularly the example sentences he had requested seem translated carefully. These were desired objects for the collection – as preserved specimens of a language, ready to be archived and subsequently researched – which he would bring to Austria as "collected" languages. Because so-called linguistic examples were deemed specimens, these were accorded a higher value for the "collection" than the recordings of so-called "free speech". In Pöch's notebook number 12, which accounts for the spoils he brought to Vienna, apart from photographs, human remains, animals and plants, "2 Hottentot languages, 10 different Bushman languages (5 ordinary)" are listed.[202] The distinction between (grammatically) free speech and example sentences in terms of treatment and reproduction is also reflected in the use of different recording methods or different methods of documentation: while the example sentences were recorded onto records, other spoken texts and songs were recorded onto wax cylinders. Specifically, these latter recordings were sparsely documented and not transcribed (see chapter 3).[203]

---

202 Pöch, notebook no. 12, p. 1110.
203 Language examples were recorded with the so-called *Archivphonograph*, which had been designed and manufactured for this purpose by the *Phonogrammarchiv* in Vienna. The records produced with this device were immediately copied in Vienna and in this way

Because example sentences and wordlists were deemed particularly important for later research, they were discussed before they were recorded. Pöch states in his protocols that the meaning of the words and sentences were checked with several speakers, and that the sentences were rehearsed before they were recorded.[204] To |Xosi Tshai Pöch attributed a "particularly clear pronunciation" of speech. It does not seem to have occurred to the anthropologist that his very clear, and perhaps also slow manner of speaking, which was intelligible for the Austrian anthropologist, may have been related to |Xosi Tshai's earlier experiences with researchers and their demands of their assistant. In the example sentences of recording ♪Ph 786, Pöch and |Kxara the Younger softly prompted the sentences which had been rehearsed already, while |Xosi Tshai was recorded. Based on this practice, I assume that the translations of the example sentences presented by Pöch in the recording protocols are at least relatively close to what was actually said. In the absence of new translations, I understand the present transcriptions of these example sentences as versions of something that was said but may have undergone a process of attenuation, which may have effected distortions and interventions. Yet among these written documents, specifically the example sentences − similar to those transcribed by Dorothea Bleek − are fragmented echoes of subaltern speech positions and comments that do not exist elsewhere.[205]

The following phrases spoken by |Xosi Tshai were recorded and archived by Pöch as "idioms [...] in contribution to the phonology and grammar of the !Ai-Khoe (Naron) language".[206] They speak of Pöch's linguistic investigations. Yet if one retracts their reduction to linguistic specimens,

became durable archival objects. Wax cylinders were recorded on a phonograph. The curator Gerda Lechleitner assumes that the cylinders were recorded in order to introduce the recording technique to the speakers. Accordingly, Pöch would have played them for the speakers and listeners. It is also conceivable that he wanted to record cylinders for the *Phonogramm-Archiv* in Berlin. The *Phonogramm-Archiv* in Berlin has 46 wax cylinder recordings that Pöch brought back from his journey to what was then German New Guinea from 1904 to 1906, see Ziegler, *Die Wachszylinder des Berliner Phonogramm-Archivs*, p. 242. The wax cylinder recordings from the Kalahari are on the CD published in 2003; they are not documented in writing. I thank Gerda Lechleitner from the *Phonogrammarchiv* Vienna for this information.

204 Protocol form for recordings Ph 797 and Ph 770.
205 *Ibid.*
206 Protocol form for recording Ph 786.

the last six of the total of twelve sentences spoken by |Xosi Tshai on recording Ph 786 read as a description of his situation that filters through the transcription:

Ich fürchte mich zu reden.
Warum lachst du?
Ich bin durstig und will Wasser.
Ich bin hungrig.
Ich bitte um Kost.
Wenn ich nichts zu
essen bekomme, sterbe ich
I'm afraid to talk.
Why are you laughing?
I am thirsty and want water.
I am hungry.
I ask for food.
If I have nothing to eat
I will die.

THE PAST, THE PRESENT AND THE DEAFNESS OF COLONIAL
KNOWLEDGE PRODUCTION

> *[...] the extreme situation of mésentente is that in which X*
> *does not see the common object presented to him by Y, because*
> *he does not hear that the sounds emitted by Y form words,*
> *and combinations of words similar to his own language.*

Jacques Rancière[207]

On August 22 and 23, 1908, voice recordings were produced with Kubi and
|Xosi Tshai. These recordings initiated Pöch's cinematographic recording with
Kubi, which would become the basis for Schüller's short film of 1984, *Busch-*
mann spricht in den Phonographen (Bushman speaks into the Phonograph). First
|Xosi Tshai spoke of the former abundance of water in the area. In what
follows, I read the sequence of narratives based on Pöch's transcripts of the
recordings. The first narrative, which engaged with the water situation of the
past, was told by the campfire; it was not acoustically documented. Pöch writes:

> *Am Abende vorher saßen viele alte Männer beim Feuer zusammen, der Ts-aukhoe Kubi*
> *(A 180) und die Ai-khoe Dsedum (A 199) Ka//tna (A 122) und Nubi. Sie erzählten*
> *von den alten Zeiten, da das Land noch wasserreicher war, und da die Elephanten in den*
> *Pfannen tranken, wühlten, und sich badeten. Tshai (|Xosi), der anwesend war, wieder-*
> *holt heute diese Erzählung für den Archiv-Phonographen. Er sagt fast mit den selben*
> *Worten, was der alte Kubi (der Älteste), am Abende vorher gesprochen hat. Er wiederholt*
> *seine kurze Erzählung dreimal. Der Beginn der Erzählung ist immer das Wort ‡kxoa*
> *(Elephanten).*

The evening before, many old men sat together by the fire, the Ts-aukhoe
Kubi (A 180) and the Ai-khoe Dsedum (A 199) Ka//tna (A 122) and Nubi.
They spoke of the old times when the land was richer in water and when
elephants drank, and bathed in the pans. Tshai (|Xosi), who was present, re-
peated this story today for the archival phonograph. He narrated this almost
in the same words as old Kubi the night before. He repeated his short story
three times. The beginning of the story is always the word ‡kxoa (elephants).[208]

---

207   Rancière, *Das Unvernehmen*, p. 11 (my translation from German).
208   Protocol form for Ph 781, parenthesis in the original.

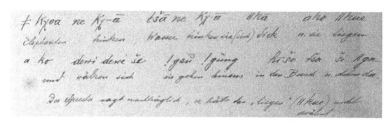

Fig. 11: Extract from the protocol form for recording Ph 781, Phonogrammarchiv, Vienna.

Pöch's summary of the first acoustic recording with |Xosi Tshai (𝔅 Ph 781), probably one of at least four versions on the same theme, which circulated in the group, reads as follows:

Elephanten trinken Wasser, trinken sie (sich) dick

u. sie liegen und wälzen sich, sie gehen hinaus in den Busch u. ?

Der Sprecher sagt nachträglich, er hätte das 'liegen' (‖ kue) nicht erwähnt.

Elephants drink water, drink them (themselves) fat

and they lie and roll, they go out into the bush and?

The speaker says afterwards that he had not mentioned the 'lying' (‖ kue).

|Xosi Tshai's narrative, which Pöch reduced to a few sentences, was re-translated after audio editing.[209] Job Morris's translation of the acoustically intelligible parts of the audio recording shows that |Xosi Tshai's spoken text was much longer than Pöch's summary, which formally mimics a transcription. 110 years after the recording, Job Morris, Naro speaker and activist for San rights from D'kar, Botswana, was able to understand the following (Ph 781, August 2018):[210]

209 Axel Rab did the sound editing of the wave file from the *Phonogrammarchiv* in summer 2018 with kind permission of the archive.

210 Ph 781. Job Morris identifies as San and is the founder of the San Youth Network, see https://sanyouthnetwork.wordpress.com, accessed March 2019. For the translation of the recordings, it is of some importance that Job Morris comes from D'kar, which is close to the location where the recordings were produced. My attempt to get a second translation by a Naro speaker from Gobabis failed because of regional language differences. The designation of Naro as a dialect cluster indicates the existence of significant language differences within the quite small group of speakers, which often hinder mutual understanding. The colonial and current borders between Namibia and Botswana may have hindered exchanges between speakers. I thank Kileni Fernando for her support and Appolia Dabe for engaging with the recordings in summer 2018.

[unclear] and become fully fed and roll over the ground. Develop a big belly and the anger goes out and the flame goes down and drink and become full and lie on the ground and roll over ... and clean with small quantity of water ... [unclear voice] ... and get out ... [unclear voice].
Wipe the mouth and go in to the wild and spend some time there ... [long pause] [unclear] ... and drink and quench my thirst and become full and lie down and roll over in the pan.
After getting out of there, I go to another bush and spend time there ... [long pause] ... and the animals come and drink and lie on the ground and roll over and go away into the bush and stay there ... and the elephants come and drink and become full and roll over the water and go away into the wild ... [unclear voice until end of recording][211]

The first recording with Kubi on this subject was also produced on the same day. On the protocol form for recording ⑨ Ph 785, Pöch writes:

Vorbemerkung:
Kubi, unter den Anwesenden der älteste Mann, und ein guter Erzähler, wiederholt seine Schilderung der Elephantenherden, welche früher bei der Pfanne seines Feldes gewohnt haben. Er hat davon zum erstenmale [sic] am vorhergehenden Abend (21 August) beim Feuer gesprochen, einen kurzen Auszug theilte Tshai (Xosi) auf Platte 781 mit. Kubi spricht in der Ts-aukhoe –Sprache, welche der !Ai-khoe Sprache sehr nahe verwandt ist.

211 I have not been able to obtain a Naro transcription for most of the translations at this stage. This is partly because Naro is written by very few of its
speakers. I am aware that the transition from a drinking elephant to a drinking
first person calls for an explanation. This transition may be specifically significant in the context of narratives in Ju/'hoan, but also in the !Xam records in
the Bleek and Lloyd Archive, in which characters are both animals (elephants,
for example) and humans (Megan Biesele, *Women Like Meat: The Folklore and Foraging Ideology of Kalahari Ju/'hoan,* Johannesburg: Wits University Press, 1993, p. 139).
At this point we have not been able to clarify these questions due to massive
gaps in the (audible) text.

Viele !Ai-Khoe können Ts-aukhoe sprechen, sie können sich gegenseitig aber auch so ziemlich gut verstehen.

Inhalt:

Kubi erzählt sehr lebhaft unter fortwährendem Mienenspiel und Handbewegungen. Er sagt, die Pfannen seien früher voll Wasser gewesen das ganze Jahr, und hätten sich immer wieder gefüllt. Die Pfanne hier, Kx-au (Kamelpan) Tsau-Kxiri („Gautsiri") und die Pfanne Kubi. Elephanten, Rhinozerosse und Büffel hätten da getrunken, in dem Wasser gebadet, gewühlt und sich darin gerollt. Stand die Sonne höher, so verließen sie das Wasser und gingen in den Busch. Die Elephantenpfade konnte man früher sehen, jetzt ist alles verwischt.

Dies ist die ungefähre Inhaltsangabe. Er wurde nur nachträglich befragt, ebenso die Umstehenden (darunter Tshai (A 198) u. mein Diener |Kxara); sonst wurde Kubi volle Freiheit gelassen.

<u>Preliminary remarks</u>:

Kubi, the eldest man among those present and a good storyteller, repeated his description of the herds of elephants that used to live near the pan of his field. He spoke of this for the first time the previous evening (August 21) at the fire. A shorter extract was given by Tshai (Xosi) on record 781. Kubi speaks in the Ts-aukhoe language, which is closely related to the !Ai-khoe language. Many !Ai-Khoe can speak Ts-aukhoe, but they can also understand each other quite well.

<u>Content:</u>

Kubi talks very vividly, with constant facial expressions and hand movements. He says that the pans used to be full of water all year round, and that they filled up again and again. The pan here, Kx-au (camel pan), Tsau-Kxiri ("Gautsiri") and the pan Kubi. Elephants, rhinos and buffaloes drank there, bathed in the water, and rolled in it. When the sun was high, they would leave the water and go into the bush. You used to be able to see the elephant tracks, but now everything is blurred.

This is the approximate summary. He was only asked [to summarize his text] afterwards, as were the bystanders (including Tshai (A 198) and my servant |Kxara); otherwise Kubi was given full freedom [of speech].

Pöch's summary is the result of "subsequent inquiry" and based on an "approximate summary". |Xosi Tshai and |Kxara most likely translated from Ts'ao khoe into Afrikaans, which was then summarized by Pöch in German. Misapprehension in the communication in Afrikaans, between

|Kxara the younger, |Xosi Tshai, and Pöch is discussed in the third chapter. Questions around the speakers' fear of the anthropologist, which |Xosi Tshai's phrase "I am afraid to speak" mentions, are also discussed in more detail in chapter 3. Here I would like to point out that it remains unclear what |Xosi Tshai and |Kxara, who both worked for Pöch, actually did convey and how these variations on a topic may have related to each other. From the recording with Kubi,[212] Job Morris was able to understand one single sentence, which does not appear in Pöch's transcripts:[213]

This is the white man's land.

Yet this singular recorded fragment, or acoustic shard, and Job Morris's translation thereof, does perturb the certainties Pöch's protocol forms seek to establish. It raises the question of whether certain content that |Kxara and |Xosi Tshai articulated was not communicated with Pöch when the recordings were translated, or whether Pöch altered the content of Kubi's spoken text. In my experience with historical recordings, which were produced in the context of colonial knowledge production, the regular omission of words and semantic meaning is neither unusual nor accidental. On the basis of the fragments we have, the question of who omitted content, and in which phase of the epistemic and archival process this actually happened, cannot be clarified.

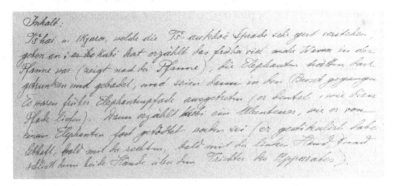

Fig. 12: Extract from the protocol form for recording Ph 789, Phonogrammarchiv Vienna.

212   Ph 785.
213   Ph 785.

On the following day, Pöch produced another recording with Kubi, whom he asked to retell the narrative for an additional phonographic recording. Pöch describes his motives for the cinematographic recording as follows:

Kubi hat bei seiner Erzählung so lebhaft in den Archiv-Phonographen gesprochen, am 22. August, so lebhaft gestikuliert, und so in den Trichter hineingesprochen, als ob er wirklich einem anderen Menschen etwas erzählen wollte, dass ich mich entschloss, diese Szene kinematographisch festzuhalten. Um alles vollständig naturgetreu zu machen, wurde auch wieder eine wirkliche Aufnahme der Erzählung mit dem Archiv-Phonographen gemacht. Da es sich aber im Wesentlichen um eine Wiederholung der im ganzen zufriedenstellenden Aufnahme auf Platte Nr. 785 handelt wurde eine minderwertige Platte eingestellt. Maßgebend war auch, dass ich während der ganzen Phonogramm Aufnahme die Kurbel des Kinematographen zu drehen und meine ganze Aufmerksamkeit der kinematograph. Aufnahme zuzuwenden hatte. Kubi mag manchmal zu laut gesprochen haben, dem Trichter zu nah gekommen sein, u.s.w.
(Die Platte 789 ist minderwertig durch tiefe Kratzer, über ihrer Oberfläche reichend, die sie schon beim Auspacken hatte. Sie war offenbar nicht fest genug im Karton gesteckt (?) u. das Wachs hatte sich am Deckel während der Erschütterungen beim Transport mit dem Ochsenwagen verkratzt).

Kubi spoke so vividly into the archive phonograph on August 22, gesticulating so vividly and speaking into the funnel as if he really wanted to communicate something to another person that I decided to record this scene cinematographically. In order to make everything completely true to life, a real recording of the narration was also recorded again with the archive phonograph. However, since this was essentially a repetition of the recording on record No. 785, which was altogether satisfactory, an inferior record was used. Another decisive factor was that I had to turn the crank of the cinematograph during the entire phonogram recording and thus had to turn my full attention to the cinematographic recording. Kubi may have spoken too loudly at times, or perhaps came too close to the funnel, and so on.
(Record 789 is inferior due to deep scratches, extending over its surface, which already existed when I unpacked it. It was obviously not wrapped tightly enough in the box (?) and the wax had scratched the lid during the transport by ox cart). [214]

214 Protocol form for Ph 789, parenthesis in the original, my emphasis.

Regarding the content of the recording, Pöch notes:

Tshai und | Kxara, welche die Ts-aukhoe Sprache sehr gut verstehen, geben an: Kubi hat erzählt, dass früher viel mehr Wasser in der Pfanne war (zeigt nach der Pfanne), die Elephanten hätten dort getrunken und gebadet, und seien dann in den Busch gegangen. Es waren früher Elephantenpfade ausgetreten (er deutet, wie diese Pfade liefen). Dann erzählt Kubi ein Abenteuer, wie er von einem Elefanten fast getötet worden sei (er gestikuliert dabei lebhaft, bald mit der rechten, bald mit der linken Hand, und schließt dann beide Hände über den Trichter des Apparates).

Tshai and | Kxara, who understand the Ts-aukhoe language very well, state: Kubi has told us that there used to be much more water in the pan (points to the pan), the elephants would have drunk and bathed there, and then went into the bush. There used to be elephant trails (he points to how these trails ran). Then Kubi tells an adventure about how he was almost killed by an elephant (he gestures animatedly, sometimes with his right hand, sometimes with his left, and then closes both hands over the funnel of the apparatus).[215]

Pöch's impression that Kubi was trying to communicate appears credible retrospectively, judging by the only sentence Job Morris was able to translate from Kubi's recording. Pöch's summary of Kubi's personal account of his perilous encounter with an elephant (which we could not hear) suggests that his narrative did not merely speak of the water conditions of the past. However, Pöch's impression that Kubi "really wanted to communicate something to another person" did not spark an attempt to understand, transcribe and translate what was said as accurately as possible on the part of the anthropologist. Nor did it prompt a conversation that would have added to Pöch's understanding of what was being communicated. Here, too, the mésentente in the recording situation surfaces: as with | Xosi Tshai's example sentences, Pöch did not consider the moment of knowledge production as an instance of communication. Rather, it was the moment in which knowledge was extracted and artefactualized, so as to become another object in Pöch's list of spoils and achievements. Clearly, Pöch did not see the speakers as interlocutors. They were deemed "native informants", objects of investigation and providers of the "raw material" of speech that was mined and taken home by means of pho-

215   *Ibid.*

nographic recording. Pöch's colonial attitude and his choices configured the archival material preserved from his Kalahari trip accordingly. To him, Kubi's attempt to communicate while speaking into the phonograph was above all a spectacle. His reaction to this was the visual capture of what he saw and did not care to listen to. As in Robert J. Flaherty's 1922 film *Nanook of the North,* in which the person with the ethnographic stage name *Eskimo* had to try to eat a record in a film scene, and as with the East Africans recorded by Karl Weule in 1906, who, according to Weule, were worried that recording would lead to a loss of voice, in this situation of colonial knowledge production, speakers were expected to express awe or fear. They were represented as savages who were not able to grasp the technology of recording sound.[216]

The comparison of the available written documentations shows that, contrary to Pöch's assessment, Kubi's accounts of 22 and 23 August are versioned narratives. Additionally, Job Morris' retranslation demonstrates that |Xosi Tshai's spoken text differs significantly from Pöch's summary. Did Pöch omit words in the written documentation? Did the two translators version the texts in translation? Did |Xosi Tshai and |Kxara leave out aspects that might have caused conflict? How different were Kubi's two versions from each other? The question of who versioned the narratives in which way – Pöch, the speakers, the translators, all of them? – or how we are to read transcriptions of "free speech" that flatly suppress the phrase, "This is the white man's land," cannot be answered on the basis of these attenuated transcripts.

To Pöch, who aimed to produce and take home specimens, the practice of versioning, and thereby creating dialogic, at times ambiguous, texts was irritating. This surfaces in his notes on "collecting" phonographic speech samples, in which he describes Kubi as an informant whose speech documents were only useful as samples of the "overall musical character of the Bushman language" because "unfortunately, this man was not at all able to adhere to a text once spoken when reproducing it". On the one

216 Katharina Sacken, "Ungern vor Fremden gesungen: Koloniale Phonographie um 1900", *Phonorama: Eine Kulturgeschichte der Stimme als Medium,* Berlin: Matthes & Seitz, 2004; see also Heike Behrend, "Ham Mukasa wundert sich: Bemerkungen zur Englandreise eines Afrikaners (1902)", Heike Behrend and Thomas Geider (eds.), *Afrikaner schreiben zurück: Texte und Bilder afrikanischer Ethnographen,* Köln: Köppe Verlag 1998; Michael Taussig, *Mimesis and Alterity: A Particular History of the Senses,* New York and London: Routledge, 1993.

hand, this is based on the assumption that statements can be made about the melody of Naro independently of the textual content.[217] Variation or dialogic[218] versioning as an aesthetic or discursive strategy, which pluralized meaning, and teased out historical facets by means of varying a theme, does not appear as a possibility in Pöch's documentation; neither can it be retrieved retrospectively in the absence of audible material.[219]

Based on Pöch's written transcripts of the audio recordings, which appear in the publication of the CD by the Austrian Academy of Sciences (2003), I assume that between the 21st and the 23rd of August, at least four corresponding narrative versions of a theme were presented by |Xosi Tshai and Kubi. Although Pöch's understanding of the texts was fragmentary at best, he claimed that the recordings Ph 781, Ph 785, and Ph 789 presented one and the same narrative, which was repeated several times. As far as the strategies of mediation through varied repetition are concerned, the loss of the acoustic recording is an absolute loss of meaning, because this discursive strategy and its nuances of developing meaning in versions are irretrievably swallowed in Pöch's summaries.

Pöch's protocol forms give no indication that he would have attended to or discerned specific genres – not even in the sense of superimposing a European generic repertoire of fables, tales or other narrative forms on the texts of the Naro speakers. Clearly the anthropologist did not expect his inquiries into a past hydrogeological situation, the wording of which we do not know, to prompt a response in particular genres of orature.

217 See Hoffmann, *Knowing By Ear.*
218 Pöch, "Technik und Wert des Sammelns", p. 12.
219 Here I use Esther Peeren's concept of *versioning* in the sense of a "continuing activity of creating versions, transforming, turning over". See "Seeing more (Hi)Stories: Versioning as Resignificatory Practice in the *What We See* Exhibition and the Work of Sanell Aggenbach and Mustafa Maluka", Anette Hoffmann (ed.), *What We See*, p. 86; Esther Peeren, *Intersubjectivities and Popular Culture: Bakhtin and Beyond,* Stanford: Stanford University Press, 2008. A good example of dialogic versioning in successive sound recordings are the recordings with the Nama speaker Haneb (whose surname is not known) on cylinders 3 and 4 and with the Otjiherero speaker Wilfred Tjiueza on cylinder 6 of the collection recorded by Hans Lichtenecker in Namibia in 1931 (*Phonogramm-Archiv* Berlin). Both tell a version of the fable of the jackal and the sun, which Hendrik Witbooi had already used as an allegory for colonization. While in Haneb's version the jackal cannot get rid of the sun, in Wilfred Tjiueza's version he shakes it off eventually. See Anette Hoffmann, "Of Storying and Storing: 'Reading' Lichtenecker's Voice Recordings", Jeremy Silvester (ed.), *Re-Viewing Resistance in Namibian History,* Windhoek: UNAM Press, 2015. See also Wessels, *Bushman Letters,* p. 76.

Carolyn Steedman has pointed to the inability of many academic researchers to hear or read genres in their interpretations of worker's narratives as "oral history", which they thus generally perceived as autobiographical accounts.[220] The narratives were thus reduced to the form of a report or personal account and stripped of any literary genre or narrative strategy. The existence of oral genres rich in metaphors, which enabled the speakers | Xosi Tshai and Kubi to refer indirectly, and perhaps melancholically, to a more affluent time, could have been known by the anthropologist, who was familiar with the fables and fairy tales from South Africa published by Wilhelm Bleek as early as 1870. Yet this possibility was apparently inconceivable to him. The unimaginable was suppressed and thus remains absent in the archive. I can therefore merely point to the potential existence of the strategic use of particular genres of spoken text,[221] and attribute retrospective significance in Trouillot's sense to these spoken texts, of which the archive has kept fragmentary traces. Accordingly, I suggest reading the transcriptions of spoken texts in the colonial archive as fragments, which acknowledges the loss of nuance and genre-specific polyphony, and the absence of the potential excess of meaning that comes with the practice of versioning that has been irreversibly lost in their reduction to written documents.[222]

Pöch's comments show that Kubi's attempt to address and perhaps discuss specific topics with the visiting anthropologist was bound to fail: Pöch was not interested in the narratives as narratives, or as a form of communicative exchange. Possible variations of a spoken text, a spectrum of meanings encapsulated in particular genres, the excess of meaning created by means of versioning, all fell into the void of his disinterest. What remains of Kubi's narratives is a faint echo of spoken texts that may have addressed the conditions of life in the past. It may have carried references to the relationship between humans and elephants; it may have spoken to

220 Carolyn Steedman, "Enforced Narratives: Stories of Another Self", Tess Cosslett, Celia Lury and Penny Summerfield (eds.), *Feminism and Autobiography: Texts, Theories, Methods*, London: Routledge 2000, p. 26.

221 Wilhelm Heinrich Immanuel Bleek, *Reineke Fuchs in Afrika: Fabeln und Märchen der Eingeborenen. Nach Original Manuskripten der Grey'schen Bibliothek in der Kap-Stadt und anderen authentischen Quellen*, Weimar: Böhlau, 1870.

222 Michel-Rolph Trouillot, *Silencing the Past*, p. 59.

a particular association of elephants with rain and water and thus, fundamentally, with life, vitality and abundance.[223]

Guenther points out that for practical and ideological reasons Naro speakers rarely hunted elephants before hunters like Charles Anderson and Frederic Green invaded the area and shot hundreds of elephants.[224] He does not mention specific ideological reasons. Megan Biesele describes the relationship of Ju/'hoan speakers to elephants as complex: On the one hand, some characters in their narratives oscillate between elephant and human. On the other hand, strong similarities between elephants and humans are also described in everyday life, which probably banned the consumption of elephant meat, at least for some Ju/'hoansi:[225]

> "Elephant? I don't eat it," said /ukxa N!a'n. "Nobody now does. It's like people's flesh and bush-animal flesh, all hanging down. It's a koaqkoaq (thing to be feared), tci dore (bad, strange thing). You don't eat it, because it is like a person, the female has two breasts and they are on her chest like a woman's".[226]

I do not mean to equate the approaches and concepts of Ju/'hoan speakers with those of Naro and Ts'aokhoe speakers, nor do I want to freeze these over a period of more than 80 years (between Pöch's and Biesele's research). I am aware that the languages are not related. Yet Ju/'hoan speakers lived under similar conditions as foragers further north, on both sides of the (present-day border) between Namibia and Botswana. The two groups use a similar system to minimize socio-economic risks (see page 138). Multilingualism, particularly in the border area, does make the exchange of stories quite possible.

Of Kubi's narration, only one sentence remains as an echo in the acoustic documents that Pöch took to Vienna from the Kalahari. It de-

---

223   For the significance of certain animals in !Xam narratives, see for instance Michael Wessel's discussion of the importance of lions in *Bushman Letters*, p. 279. In recent years, it has become known to Western researchers that elephants can perceive waterholes at a distance of up to five kilometers and also notice rain at an even greater distance, which was known to foragers and contributes to the connection of elephants and water in their narrative and conceptual repertoire.

224   Guenther, "'Lords of the Desert Land'", p. 125.

225   Biesele, *Women Like Meat*, p. 139.

226   *Ibid.*, p. 150.

scribes the dramatic changes that Naro and Ts'aokhoe speakers faced in Ghanzi: already before Pöch pitched his tent on a white farmer's land and travelled with the camels of the *Schutztruppe*, their home had become the land of the whites. Pöch's question about the hydrogeological conditions in the Kalahari resounds with Passarge's interests. Passarge writes:

Ich bedaure sehr, nicht selbst gleichfalls die Buschmänner nach der Entstehung der Pfan- nenkrater im Chansefeld gefragt zu haben. Sie hätten vielleicht noch interessante Mit- teilungen auf Grund früherer direkter Beobachtungen machen können, z.B. mein treuer Begleiter Koschep, in dessen Gegenwart der letzte Elephant des Chansefeldes von dem Jäger Robinson geschossen wurde.

I very much regret not having asked the Bushmen about the formation of the pan craters in the *Chansefeld.* They might have been able to give interest- ing information based on their direct observations, e.g. my faithful compan- ion Koschep, in whose presence the last elephant of the Chansefeld was shot by the hunter Robinson.[227]

Unfortunately, it is unclear what Pöch noted about the production of the sound recordings, since his notebooks from the period during which they were produced have been lost. It is likely that Pöch tried to follow up on Passarge's research; how exactly he communicated this question, how this was understood by the speakers, and in which genres they answered remains unclear. As with the vast majority of historical audio recordings produced by anthropologists or linguists, the requests to speak or specifi- cations of topics for the recordings do not appear in the transcripts. The phrase "This is the white man's land," and the fragments that Job Morris translated from these narratives of the abundance of water, perhaps dur- ing the time before cattle holders had moved in and the water table sank, refer to the loss of water and, ultimately, a corresponding loss of affluence for foragers in the area of the Ghanzi Ridge. Dialogically, through several speakers, perhaps over several days, a dramatic change was probably dis- cussed, in a way that pointed to factors beyond hydrogeological conditions.

---

227 Passarge, *Die Buschmännner der Kalahari*, p. 341.

THE ETERNAL "BUSHMAN"

Dietrich Schüller's short film from 1984, which synchronized Pöch's cine-matographic recording with the acoustic recording, focused on a technical achievement: the historical moment of the double ethnographic recording produced by Pöch. The film thus stages Pöch's position as a pioneer of eth-nographic film and sound recording. For this, Schüller chose the damaged second recording (Ph 789) as the soundtrack. Schüller's selection shows his interest in the authenticity of the moment of the recording. He identified Pöch as the author of the archival objects, and thus also of the sound re-cording. In this production, Kubi's narrative is swallowed in favour of the spectacle of the cinematographic documentation of a sound recording in the Kalahari. The spoken narrative was as irrelevant in the moment of the original film recording as it was in the written documentation and in the moment of the fusing of the historical film and the sound recording (al-most) 80 years later. Schüller's clip thus repeats the silencing of the speaker in the very moment of the cinematographic sound recording. The film, which continues to circulate on the web, transports these selections to the present.

Schüller's film document has been critically reviewed several times – mostly addressing the cinematographic documentation of a staged juxta-position of the "primitive" with the (then) new technologies of sound and film recording. The Namibian historian Robert Gordon, known for his work on the representation of *Bushmen*, rightly points to the collaborative moment of the staging of *Bushman-ness*: It was not Pöch alone who staged the figure of the *Bushman*. In the situation of filming, the speaker was not only an object but also an actor.[228] Yet how voluntarily this happened remains unclear. Gordon also assumes that those who were depicted as *Bushmen* may have been un/dressed for the purpose of producing photo-graphs in order to create the impression of "authentic primitives".[229] Britta Lange[230] and Assenka Oksiloff[231] have also discussed the disappearance of Kubi's spoken text – which was overwritten by the visual figure of the *Bushman*. Oksiloff's assessment that the words are *not* lost but could be

---

228 Gordon, "'Captured on Film': Bushmen and the Claptrap of the Performative Primi-tive", Paul S. Landau and Deborah D. Kaspin (eds.), *Images and Empires: Visuality in Colonial and Postcolonial Africa*, Berkeley, Los Angeles and London: University of Cali-fornia Press 2002.

229 *Ibid.*, p. 216.

230 Lange, *Die Wiener Forschungen an Kriegsgefangenen*, pp. 311–316.

231 Oksiloff, *Picturing the Primitive*.

reconstructed from Pöch's notes and thus added to the cinematographed speech scene afterwards can be rejected on the basis of my study.

The film reinscribes an opaque representation which creates the figure of *Bushman*, whose silhouette emerges from the fog of an old cinematographic recording, and who is, again, depicted as ultimately other. The language barrier is represented by impenetrable noise, the focus on visual appearance, the gesticulations with no legible meaning, all of which assert (or repeat) the absence of intelligible speech. The absence of subtitles or explanations of the text in the film reinforces the impression of untranslatability, of semantic obscurity. The film depicts colonial epistemic practices as *autopsia* – which is knowing the other as seeing with one's own eyes. The short film shows a man who speaks but communicates nothing, his gestures emptied without words. Noise has drowned out articulation, forever repeating the impossibility of understanding what he said. The speaker becomes the obscure object of Western curiosity. As with the measurements, the mouldings, the theft and trade in their remains, the object *Bushman*, always already categorized, is subjected to autopsy: to exploration, imaging and description based on seeing and *only* on the seeing of others.

The exact wording of Kubi's narratives has not been preserved because the first acoustic recording was poor and the second was not heard in the silent movie. A precise transcription and translation were not needed, since Pöch expected a response to a question about the hydrogeology of the area, and had no use for a dialogic, versioned text, or variations of narratives that unfolded in polyphony. The result of this deafness to the dialogic historiography of those already defined as *Bushmen*, which began with Pöch but does not end with him, was not so much an abrupt, accidental loss of words. Rather it was a process of attenuation in several steps, in which meaning was lost gradually. This gradual attenuation was caused by the use of a broken record as much as by the absence of an accurate transcription or translation, by the repetition of word deafness in synchronization 80 years after the recording, up to the point of irreversible loss of the words. The only sentence that Job Morris could trawl from the noisy recording was once part of a swarm of communicating utterances, which had since lost its resonance and had become ossified, pointing to a lost body of narratives that spoke of irreversible change caused by colonial capture, uttered on August 23, 1908 in what is now Kg'au tshàa, northeast of Ghanzi, by a speaker we know only by the name Kubi: "This is the white man's land."

Fig. 13: |Kxara dressed up, photographed by Rudolf Pöch.

3 ECHOES OF FEAR AND THE ANTHROPOLOGIST AS "BUSHMAN"

*[...] what we are observing here is archival power at its
strongest, the power to define what is, and what is not a
serious object of research and, therefore, of mention.*

Michel-Rolph Trouillot[232]

In historiography, it matters who speaks. This concerns writing positions
as much as it does available acoustic sources. Practices and processes of
archival selection have *de facto* determined what is, or is not, available for
the writing of historiographies in the present.[233] During processes of
colonial knowledge production with audile technologies,[234] researchers
produced objects, which they planned to archive themselves, or to hand
over to sound archives, which may have commissioned the recordings
and equipped researchers with the devices to record. The recordings were
then archived in line with what was perceived to be pertinent material for
the researcher's own investigations, the aims of the archive, but also in
line with what were imagined to be relevant topics for later studies. Archives may have conserved, altered, discarded or lost the documents they
received.[235] In the case of this particular acoustic collection, Pöch produced the recordings in Ghanzi with Naro speakers and he subsequently
archived them himself at the *Phonogrammarchiv* in Vienna after he returned
to Austria in 1909. He was in the position to control the process of recording, he selected most of what was recorded, how it was recorded and with
whom, and controlled the subsequent processes of documentation and
conservation. This means that although the *Phonogrammarchiv* in Vienna
had an interest in language recordings from the Kalahari, and had provided Pöch with the technical equipment and the pre-printed protocol forms
to record and document language samples, it was nevertheless Pöch who

---

232 Trouillot, *Silencing the Past*, p. 99.
233 *Ibid.*
234 Sterne, *The Audible Past.*
235 Hamilton, "Forged and Continually Refashioned".

decided which recordings would be documented in which way, and how these were filed.

Apart from questions around archival efficacy, there is also the question of how particular recorded documents speak. The excess of voice, which always speaks beyond words, is able to transmit additional meaning, or acoustic content, in sound. Crucially, voice can and does communicate beyond, or even despite, written documentation. Historical sound recordings make audible that it not only matters who spoke, but also through which archival object, or particular medium we hear, or read sources of colonial history.

One of the recordings discussed in this chapter shows that, in terms of the power of archives and (then) contemporary narratives of colonial knowledge production, the choice of objects or sources matters, even if this choice does not entail a change in speakers, but only a shift of speaking positions. As with photographs, historical sound recordings often reveal topics or events that did not enter the written record but may be of interest or significance retrospectively. Moreover, the difference between what is recorded acoustically and what is available in writing allows the effects of archival power to surface. Thus, listening to historical sound recordings may enable researchers to piece together more complex reconstructions of situations or events. This also may alter our understandings of the positions of speakers. Listening closely to sound recordings may shift what we as listeners hear as relevant topics, challenge our preconceived notions of what mattered to the speakers, or bring up issues pertinent in the present. Because recordings may not be well documented (or the understanding of what this would entail may have shifted) but still exist as acoustic documents, it becomes possible to attend to speech acts that may have become significant only recently and only because the recordings are now understood as historical sources and not merely as linguistic specimens.

This chapter engages with two recordings produced in the Kalahari in 1908, of which the first one (⅋Ph 792) exists only as an acoustic record, audible on the CD yet not listed in the contents of this CD. In the second recording (⅋Ph 763), the recorded speech content was released from its limiting categorization as an object of knowledge for linguistic research by means of Job Morris' recent translation. Both recordings highlight the difference between acoustic recordings and their written documentation, drawing attention to the fragmentary nature of the acoustic documents as snippets of conversations and acoustic shards that speak of colonial knowledge production. For Pöch, Ph 792 was a recording of no epistemic value, which subsequently disappeared from the written register. Recording Ph 763 was documented and archived as a linguistic recording, that is, as part of a "collection of languages" that Pöch proudly included in the list of spoils he was able to carry off to Vienna.[236] Ph 763 was recorded as an example of free speech in Naro. These differences in archival registration and subsequent curatorial care may seem paradoxical, yet they follow the logic of colonial linguistics, which mostly had no interest in the semantic content of speech or the intentions of speakers. Both recordings speak from the scene of performing for the phonograph. They transmit information on the status of the speakers in the project, and contain traces of the scene of colonial knowledge production. Yet they also speak of the intentions and practices of the anthropologist, which have been outlined in the previous chapter of this book. In the case of the two recordings discussed below, the "thingification" of the speech acts (Césaire's *chosification*) at the moment of preservation, which turns speech into a recording, and the successive disappearance of these same spoken words from the archive becomes apparent: what is audible on the recordings does not correspond with Pöch's written documentation.[237] For those who do not understand Naro, the second recording becomes apprehensible by means of Job Morris's translation.

Attending to the conditions of colonial knowledge production, together with the power relations that become audible with the recordings, allows us to listen to sound recordings as attenuated fragments of conversations which were warped or obscured in the writings of the Austrian anthropologist. Listening closely to these recordings in the present, I hear them as fragments of conversations whose torn, distant echoes reach the present only in aural form. Job Morris's retranslation, and our attention to performative and semantic content, show that the loss of words is a

---

236   In Pöch's notebook no. 12, p. 1110, he lists 10 *Bushman* languages (*Buschmannsprachen*) and 2 Nama dialects (*Hottentottensprachen*) among objects, recordings, photographs, human remains, and other items.

237   See Aimé Césaire, *Über den Kolonialismus,* Aus dem Französischen, mit einer Vorbemerkung und Anmerkungen von Heribert Becker, Berlin: Alexander Verlag, [1959] 2017.

regular symptom of colonial epistemic practices. This means that as historical sources these recordings are fragments. They may or may not reveal what listeners in the present are interested in hearing. Yet for Pöch, as a collector of languages as specimens, these recordings were perfect objects: they captured speech in languages that were of interest in Austria. Pöch's language recordings created acoustic word lists that are comparable to, for example, the written lists of words which were brought to Germany a century earlier, for instance by missionaries. Yet, while for instance Hinrich Lichtenstein, who published such a list of words,[238] was sure that Europeans could neither articulate nor document in writing what, for instance, Koranna speakers said, Pöch was able to capture acoustic speech samples verbatim with the new technique of phonographic recording.[239]

GIBBERISH AND DANGER

On the undated recording Ph 792, recorded in Kxau [Kg'au tshàa], I hear a male speaker uttering a crude mix of English, German, Dutch and Afrikaans with a thick Austrian accent:

> We bring some wood for fire and then we go to the pit to drink some water, you know ...?
>
> |Kxara, waar is die |Kxara? ...
>
> |Kxara, môre vroeg jy moet mich wakker maak
>
> Als die zon uitkomt ik moet wakker sein
>
> Is julle bang?
>
> Denkt die |Kxara ik wil die |Kxara fressen?
>
> Filos! Filos, you come!
>
> Filos, did you look after the horse?
>
> ... The bush ... very far
>
> You look at it that it niet hardloop

---

238   *Reisen im südlichen Africa*, 1812.
239   Pöch's notebooks for the time period in which the language recordings were produced are missing. Clemens Gütl (*Phonogrammarchiv Wien*), who tried to trace the missing notebooks, believes it is possible that they were used by Johannes Lukas (1901-1980) in the course of his linguistic research, and that they were not returned to Vienna afterwards. Katarina Matiasek (*Departmant für Evolutionäre Anthropologie*, University of Vienna) also researched the whereabouts of the notebooks and was unable to locate them. I thank both of them for the information.

We bring some wood for the fire and then we go to the waterhole and drink
some water, you know?
| Kxara, where is the | Kxara?
| Kxara, tomorrow morning you have to wake me up
When the sun comes out, I have to be awake
Are you afraid?
Does the | Kxara think I want to eat the | Kxara?
Filos, Filos you come [here]!
Filos, did you take care of/look after the horse?
... the bush ... far away
You make sure it doesn't run away!

The booklet accompanying the CDs published by the *Phonogrammarchiv* did
not prepare me for hearing the Austrian anthropologist speak. After years
of studying recording situations, listening in on situations of knowledge
production preserved on scratchy wax cylinders, hearing authoritarian announcements, but also laughter, coughing, clearing of throats, the tone of
voices, the words and the pauses of the speakers whose languages were
of interest to researchers, and whose bodies had often been subjected to
anthropometric examinations too, I now heard, for the first time, an anthropologist who did not merely announce the content of the following
recording, but who appears as the only speaker on this recording. Since no
other German-speaking man with a strong Austrian accent was present
during the recording sessions in Ghanzi, I assume that this is the voice of
Rudolf Pöch.

Did | Kxara, who was addressed here, understand Pöch's gibberish?
Who was Filos?[240] On the recording one hears Pöch speak a startling mix
of Afrikaans, Dutch, English and German, which probably exceeded the
regular plasticity of Afrikaans (or Cape Dutch) or English spoken in *border-
lands*.[241] Paul Landau's question of who understood exactly what, or whom,
in these regions of acute colonial power struggle, of proselytising, trade,
and colonial appropriation, and what meaning the listeners could make or

---

240 I have not been able to find a person named Filos anywhere else in the documentation.
241 On the plasticity of Afrikaans see for instance Ana Deumert, *Variation and Standardi-
     sation: The Case of Afrikaans (1880-1922)*, Cape Town: University of Cape Town Press,
     1999.

wanted to draw from what was said, resonates here.[242] Listening to Pöch's gibberish on the CD certainly shatters his claim of his own linguistic competence. It also brings up the question of how exactly he communicated with people in the area of whom the majority did not speak German. The recording sounds staged. After sound editing, which takes out some of the scratches and reduces the hiss, I listened to it with Rosemary Lombard, who understands Afrikaans better than I do, in Cape Town in December 2018.[243] Sound editing did not, as it often cannot, restore the content on the acoustic record: some words remain unintelligible. The intonation is striking. Pöch's emphasis on words in English and Afrikaans sounds exaggerated. The recording does not explain its own existence. Why did the anthropologist speak these sentences, and why did he record himself? Gerda Lechleitner, musicologist and former curator at the *Phonogrammarchiv* in Vienna, assumes that Pöch travelled with two recording devices for two different purposes. With the so-called *Archivphonograph*, he recorded speech on records for posterity. The smaller phonograph that recorded on wax cylinders but could also play back the recordings immediately, was useful to demonstrate the operation of the recording device and to give listeners the opportunity to hear themselves speak. Pöch's recording of his own voice on a wax cylinder may have been in order to stage the technique of phonography.

On the recording Ph 792, the much-discussed systematic infantilization and emasculation of African men as servants or, in colonial jargon, as "boys", becomes acoustically perceptible.[244] Pöch speaks to |Kxara, whose support was crucial for Pöch's expedition in several respects, as to a young child, with a particularly condescending intonation and speech emphasis. Here, voice, speech cadences and prosodic performance reveal what a transcription would have been unable to communicate: the hierarchy of colonial knowledge production that resounds on an acoustic recording. Fear, which Pöch does not mention in his writings about his journey, surfaces as an issue. It appears as a topic and an element of colonial knowledge production in his spoken text, recorded by himself.

242   Landau, *Popular Politics*, p. 80.
243   I thank Rosemary Lombard, DJ and language editor of this book, for checking the spelling in Afrikaans (which I mostly understand but cannot write) in the recording I transcribed. I thank Dag Henrichsen for his comments on this recording.
244   See Hoffmann and Mnyaka, "Hearing Voices in the Archive".

One can only hear the anthropologist's question: *Are you afraid?* On this particular recording the roles are reversed from what they are in most of the other recordings: the voice of the anthropologist appears as the echo; one can hear what might have been his response to an earlier action or a question by |Kxara. Despite this partial change of speaking positions, the arrangement of roles for the practice of colonial knowledge production remain set in place: Pöch asks the questions, but no answer is heard here. Neither |Kxara's response nor the motivation for Pöch's question resound directly in the acoustic documentation. Nor do the written records that stem from Pöch's journey provide an answer. Why did Pöch ask |Kxara and Filos whether they were afraid? Why did he ask |Kxara, jokingly, whether the latter thinks that Pöch might intend to devour him? How did |Kxara understand this joke, which translates the flippant German expression, "*Ich werd dich schon nicht fressen!*", when it was uttered by a man who had desecrated graves, prepared human remains of farmworkers for shipping, and obviously collaborated with the military and the colonial administration?

While Pöch recorded the speech samples on records and documented them following the request of the archive, he apparently did not deem the wax cylinders to be relevant language examples, and so the documentation of these recordings is sparse. The protocol form for Ph 792 states that this is recording number 6 of the wax cylinders, recorded in 1908 in Kxau [Kg'au tshàa] and transferred onto record at the Vienna *Phonogrammarchiv* in 1910. It also reads "Tribe: Bushmen, language of the Bushmen". The remaining headings in the protocol form remained blank. In the booklet of the CD, the only information on this recording is: "Speech, spoken by Bushmen" (CD 1, track 20). When and how did the anthropologist become a *Bushman*? According to Gerda Lechleitner, Pöch archived the recordings himself while he was employed as an assistant at the *Phonogrammarchiv* from 1909.

In this case, the archive has swallowed words almost entirely. Did no one listen to these recordings in the 108 years that have passed since they were recorded? Did the description "Speech spoken by *Bushmen*" trigger spontaneous word-deafness? As all other descriptions with which Pöch had labelled the recordings, these were apparently transferred unchecked into the booklet published with the CD of 2003. The curator I spoke to about the recording in December 2018 was surprised to hear that Pöch had recorded himself. She had not been aware that this recording could be heard on the CD released by the *Phonogrammarchiv*. This example, in which the anthropologist – at least according to the written documentation – is turned into a *Bushman*, demonstrates, perhaps more clearly than other recordings, the word deafness of the archive. What does not appear in writing seems to fade away. Yet colonial knowledge production regularly sounds different to how it reads. At times, listening to recordings that no one may have heard since they were produced can shift our understanding of the audio documents significantly, because recorded voices or words resurface that the written documentation of the colonial archive has absented.

ǀKXARA THE YOUNGER

Archival power determines what can be known of Pöch's assistants and how persons involved in his research were represented or absented. Those who were studied, which included ǀKxara, who was subjected to Pöch's research, had little influence on decisions that shaped their own presence in the colonial archive. Nor did ǀKxara participate in the design of the research topics. ǀKxara the Younger is one of three people who appear under this name.

Fig. 14: ǀKxara the Younger, next to the phonograph, and two female listeners with a child.

As with other names of people and places that appear in Pöch's diaries, the reports to the academy and the documentation of this collection, his name may have been misspelled. The archive does not allow for correction of these possible distortions retrospectively. The first man with the name |Kxara who appears in Pöch's records was "merely" examined.[245] Another speaker, who features in the fourth chapter of this book and whom Pöch called "Ou |Kxara" (old |Kxara), is described by Pöch as a loquacious speaker. I will therefore refer to the speaker whom Pöch called his cook and servant as "|Kxara the Younger". In order to come closer to answering the question of why |Kxara the Younger should or could have been afraid, it would be helpful to know from what juncture he had been travelling with Pöch. This is not entirely clear in Pöch's written records and statements, in part because Pöch systematically downplays his assistant's crucial role in the expedition. |Kxara's voice can be heard on recordings Ph 761, 762, 763 and 778. Recording Ph 761 was produced in Kxau [Kg'au tshàa] on 27 July, according to the archival record.[246]

This first recording with |Kxara the Younger preserves calls and shouts, which Pöch describes as the cries of the ox-drivers. On the protocol form for the recording Pöch writes:

Von Kxau-tsa nach Kx-au (Kamelpan) besorgte das Geschäft des Treibens meist mein Koch und Diener, der Buschmann |Kxara. Von ihm rührt obige Aufnahme her. |Kxara ist ein „domestizierter" Buschmann, der schon seit seiner frühesten Jugend im Dienste von Weißen (Engländern und Buren) steht. Er spricht außer seiner Muttersprache (Naro) die Sprache der Kau-kau Buschmänner, Nama (hottentottisch), Betschuana (Sprache der Betschuanen) und das afrikanische Holländisch.

From Kxau-tsa to Kx-au (Camelpan), the business of driving was mostly done by my cook and servant, the Bushman |Kxara. The recording was taken with him. |Kxara is a "domesticated" Bushman who has been in the service of white people (Englishmen and Boers) since his earliest youth. Apart from his mother tongue (Naro), he speaks the language of the Kau-kau Bushmen, Nama (Hottentot), Betschuana (language of the Betschuans) and African Dutch [my translation, brackets in the original].

245 Pöch, notebook no. 2, p. 177
246 Protocol form for recording Ph 761.

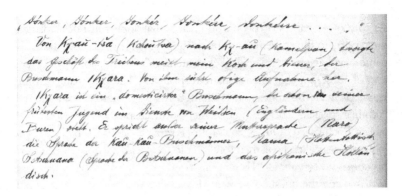

Fig. 15: Extract from the protocol form for recording Ph 761, Phonogrammarchiv, Vienna.

According to Pöch, |Kxara the Younger spoke five languages. That he was more than just a servant and cook for Pöch surfaces in the protocol forms for the recordings (*Protokolle*) and shows in the photographs that were first published and associated with the audio recordings in the German version of this book (2020): |Kxara translated for Pöch, drove the trek oxen for the wagon, and most certainly also cared for the animals. He was acoustically recorded, measured and also operated the phonograph himself while Pöch was filming (see Fig. 14). A photograph showing |Kxara with two women and a baby, listening to the phonograph, has already been published in the booklet that comes with *Kalahari Recordings*. Due to the separation of archival objects in various repositories, |Kxara the Younger was not identified as a speaker nor as Pöch's assistant by the *Phonogrammarchiv*. The photograph published in the CD booklet does not refer to him.[247] For recording Ph 775, Pöch describes another situation in which he cinematographically recorded the scene of a phonographic recording (to my knowledge, this scene has not been preserved as a film):

> *Mein Diener, der !Ai-Buschmann |Kxara (a 178) bringt den Apparat herbei, ruft die Weiber, setzt den Apparat in Gang, überwacht das Singen der Weiber, stellt den Apparat ab, entlässt die Weiber.*
>
> My servant, the !Ai Bushman |Kxara (a 178) brings the apparatus, calls the women, starts the apparatus, supervises the singing of the women, turns off the apparatus, dismisses the women.

247 Schüller (ed.), *Rudolf Pöch's Kalahari Recordings*, p. 46.

So instead of marvelling at the wondrous technology of recording, or being afraid of the phonograph, |Kxara operated the recording device, directed the speakers and also translated for Pöch in the recording situation and/or afterwards.[248] Pöch's description corresponds with Fig. 14 as well as with the staging of his research in front of his tent in Fig. 8. Pöch's description of |Kxara as a "domesticated *Bushman*" allowed him to exploit |Kxara in two respects: as a "remnant" from the past and thus a subject of his study, and as an underpaid assistant and translator in the colonial present. This also means that |Kxara's position vis-à-vis Pöch, but also vis-à-vis the other Naro speakers, was at best ambiguous.

In the protocol forms for recording Ph 778, Pöch states that |Kxara, who spoke the so-called Cape Dutch in addition to four other languages, assisted him with the clarification of linguistic terms and thus supported Pöch's research with his expertise, sharing knowledge with Pöch that was crucial for the project of recording languages. Following Pöch's narrative closely, the text in the booklet that accompanies the CD omits |Kxara's work and expertise for the second time. The indication of the number "a 178" in brackets (see quote above) refers to the examination and measurement of his body.[249]

The prefabricated protocol form issued by the *Phonogrammarchiv* in Vienna stipulated that recordists clarify and document details about the speakers of the recordings that were of use for research and classification of the recorded languages. The question on the form pertaining to "the origin of the father/mother"[250] points to linguists' interest in the genealogies and uses of languages and dialects of those who were recorded.

248   For the invitation to Africans to wonder about Europe's technical achievements, see Behrend, "Ham Mukasa wundert sich".

249   The possibility that a strand of his hair was taken or that a plaster cast was made of his body also exists. Some hair samples of the people Pöch examined are kept, as far as I know, in the *Naturhistorisches Museum* in Vienna. Plaster casts are also kept there or at the *Department für Evolutionäre Anthropologie* at the University of Vienna. The documentation of the measurements seem to be missing. See Jannik Franzen, *Bilder der „Anderen", geformt am Schillerplatz: Rassistische Forschungen an Kriegsgefangenen im Ersten Weltkrieg und die Akademie der bildenden Künste Wien*, unpublished MA thesis, *Akademie der bildenden Künste Wien*, 2019.

250   The question about the origin and language of the parents was standard and served to understand European dialects as well. It is also a component of the questionnaires of the *Königlich Preußische Phonographische Kommission*, which produced linguistic recordings with prisoners of war of the First World War in German camps. See Hoffmann, *Knowing By Ear*.

Fig. 16: | Kxara the Younger.

| Kxara was the only speaker whose parents are mentioned by Pöch in these protocol forms: according to this information, | Kxara's parents came from the vicinity of Kg'au tshàa, as did | Kxara himself. Pöch's failure to deliver the required information for the other speakers appears as a gap, which indicates that Pöch was probably unable to communicate these questions to most of the Naro speakers he recorded.[251]

The anthropologist would have been able to communicate this question to | Xosi Tshai, his other assistant, because he spoke Afrikaans and was presumably used to the gibberish of travelling hunters, traders, military men and adventurers. Yet the protocol forms of | Xosi Tshai's speech recordings do not contain any information about the origin of his parents. Since he, like | Kxara, is described as having been in the service of white hunters, travellers and farmers since childhood, it is possible that he either did not know his parents or was not willing to share this information with Pöch.

In Pöch's photographic collection, | Kxara the Younger appears in at least five photographs (see Fig. 8, 13, 14, 16 and 18). The photographs also show him as a man with an apparent zest for dressing up or trying on different styles of clothing. In the following picture, as in Fig. 13, he is wearing a loose shirt, a kind of sarong, a towel wrapped around his head, and a belt as a chest ornament. In the photograph that shows him standing in front of a tent, he appears to be wearing the same fur hat

<hr>

251 For instructions on "phonographic collecting" see for instance Bernhard Ankermann, *Anleitung zum ethnographischen Beobachten und Sammeln,* Berlin: Georg Reimer Verlag, 1914; von Luschan, "Pygmäen und Buschmänner"".

Fig. 17: Military station in Rietfontein, 1908.

that |Kxara the Elder wears in two photographs (Fig. 21 and Fig. 22).[252] I can only speculate about how exactly these moments of dressing up, or dressing for photographs, came about. In his notebooks, Pöch mentions a moment of dressing up and blackfacing for a costume ball in Las Palmas, on 30 November 1908, on his voyage to South Africa. He writes that he painted his face black and wore a costume he described as "Javanese *pakean tidar*".[253] How and why |Kxara came to dress up in a similar fashion remains uncertain.

Another question concerns from what date and for how long |Kxara was Pöch's assistant. Pöch states that on his "camel expedition" from Rietfontein, where he stayed for six weeks (from 1 May to 12 June 1908), to "Sidoni-Tsaup", from 6 to 8 June 1908 he was accompanied "by two horsemen from the station for cover" as well as a "native interpreter" (*ein einheimischer Dolmetsch*). In one of his reports to the Academy, Pöch writes:[254]

252 Pöch's photographs show that items of clothing were exchanged between the people who were present: The fur hat is worn by |Kxara the Elder and |Kxara the Younger; a pair of shoes with a bulging toe was worn by |Xosi Tshai and |Kxara the Younger.
253 Pöch, notebook no. 1, p. 7. I thank Jannik Franzen for this reference.
254 Pöch, "Berichte an die Akademie", 1908, p. 435. "Sidoni-Tsaup" or "Sidonitsaup" is one of the garbled place names that appear in the colonial archive and which could not be located on the basis of these names.

*Eine besondere Förderung erfuhren meine Studien durch den Leiter der Station Riet-
fontein, Leutnant Hans Kaufmann. Um es mir zu ermöglichen, auch die im Durstfelde
sitzenden Buschleute zu sehen, stellte er eine Kamelpatrouille zusammen. Ziel der Expedition war die 125 km von Riefontein gelegenen Wasserstelle Sidoni-Tsaup. Ich kam so in
das Sandfeld, nordwestlich von Olifantskloof.*

My studies were supported especially by the head of the Rietfontein station,
Lieutenant Hans Kaufmann. To enable me to see the bushmen living in the
Thirstland, he organised a camel patrol. The expedition's destination was the
waterhole in Sidoni-Tsaup, 125 km from Rietfontein. In this way I was able
to get to the Sandveld, northwest of Olifantskloof.[255]

Since Pöch left Rietfontein to go to Ghanzi only four days later, on 12
June 1908, and states that |Kxara led his draught oxen on this journey, I
assume that |Kxara the Younger was this translator. In the documentation
for Ph 763 with |Kxara, Pöch notes that |Kxara spoke about their arrival
in Kxau.

While |Xosi Tshai speaks of forced labour and his exploitation as
Pöch's assistant, the anthropologist does not discuss the working conditions of his assistants. The anthropologist Walter Hirschberg would later
mention in his discussion of the results of Pöch's travels that "at the end
of the week the servants received one to two plates [of tobacco]" and
were fed.[256] Hirschberg goes on to write that a slab of tobacco and a box
of matches "were considered a day's wages at that time".[257] For whom exactly this was acceptable as a daily wage – for those categorized as *Bushmen;*
for all black inhabitants of the Kalahari; for whites as well? – Hirschberg
does not specify. Why Pöch, who kept meticulous lists of his own costs
and expenses in his notebooks, found it appropriate to pay his assistants
exclusively in kind, he does not relate.[258]

255 *Ibid.*
256 Walter Hirschberg, *Völkerkundliche Ergebnisse der südafrikanischen Reisen,* p. 1.
257 *Ibid.*; Plankensteiner, *"Auch hier gilt die Regel",* p. 101.
258 In her notebooks, Dorothea Bleek describes paying for conversations and for photo-
     graphing people with tobacco and headscarves. Apparently she also traded a skeleton for
     food: "Used one tin sardine. Two tins of beef, sold coffee and tobacco, tea - got Bushman
     skeleton, butter, milk (?) coffee. [...] gave woman 4 duks [doek, Afrikaans for head-
     scarf], man tobacco for conversation and picture". Records from October 1911, in the
     area of Witdraai, see http://lloydbleekcollection.cs.uct.ac.za/books/BC_151_A3_04/
     A3_4_222.html, accessed January 2021. For Dorothea Bleek's research in 1911, see
     Bank, "Anthropology and Fieldwork Photography".

The first recording that Pöch produced with |Kxara the Younger is dated 27 July 1908 in the transcription. Unlike |Xosi Tshai, |Kxara can be heard as a speaker only on few recordings. In the protocol form for recording Ph 763, Pöch writes: "When |Kxara speaks quickly and carelessly, he mixes Nama [*Hottentottisch* in the original] words into his mother tongue (Naro), as this language is used as a means of communication among different tribes of the Kalahari Bushmen."[259] In addition, Pöch felt able to determine that |Kxara did not pronounce the "clicks clearly enough". The actual contents of

Fig. 18: Portrait |Kxara without headdress.

the recording, which Pöch claims was the first attempt to produce a Naro language recording, he only paraphrased and did not transcribe, as with almost all his recordings of so-called free speech. Pöch writes:

Diese Platte wurde zum ersten Versuche einer Buschmannsprache verwendet, um zu sehen, wie die Schnalzlaute [heraus?] kommen. Absichtlich wurde die freie Rede gewählt, mit Verzicht auf eine genaue Transkription. |Kxara gibt an, er habe über unsere Ankunft in Kxau gesprochen, über die Arbeiten mit den Buschleuten, sowie darüber, dass sie mit Tabak beschenkt warden.

This record was used for the first attempt at a Bushman's language to see how the clicks [come out?] Free speech was deliberately chosen, *with no accurate transcription*. |Kxara states that he spoke about our arrival in Kxau, about the work with the Bushmen, and about them being given tobacco.[260]

As with Kubi's spoken texts, Pöch again "refrains" (*verzichtete*) from delivering an exact transcription here. To what extent this "refraining" (*Verzicht*)

259 My translation from German.
260 Protocol form for recording Ph 763 (my emphasis and translation from German).

actually circumscribes his inability to provide an exact translation remains unclear. Yet with this statement, Pöch declared the exact content of what |Kxara said to be irrelevant for the study of the Naro language. The fact that the summary Pöch provided does not reflect |Kxara's spoken words surfaces with Job Morris' translation 100 years later, in August 2018. Due to the sound quality, Job Morris could not understand all the words, but translated the Ph 763 recording as follows:

[...] then you all run away? Is sex bad for you? [voices unclear to hear here]
[...] you all think he doesn't have gifts/presents?
You think we are all not tired [...] and instead of smoking, you run away?
Drink some tea inside that leather [...]
Instead of you accepting gifts, you run away? I thought he came here because of you [...] [unclear and static voices here] and he wants one of you.
He told me that he doesn't kill people.
[switches to another topic]
Is this leather rotten? I can smell it. It has been messed up and just brought here now. All the time we live in the wild but you don't know how to make things properly [...].
[static and unclear until the end of record]

The beginning of the translation is confusing. The words |Kxara spoke a century ago reach the present as an echo: abbreviated; fragmented; certainly out of context. When I asked Job Morris how he translated "is sex bad for you?", he explained that he understood "gae qam" ("sexual intercourse with each other") and could hear "ku sa x'oe tuue" ("against it" or actually "allergic to it"). This somewhat uncertain beginning of the translatable text of the recording may relate to gifts that were offered by the anthropologist. The question "are you (also) allergic to sex?", may jokingly refer to the rejection of gifts.

Before Job Morris, Joram Useb, who works at the *San Culture and Heritage Centre !Khwa ttu* in Yzerfontein (South Africa),[261] listened to the

---

261   *!Khwa ttu* in Yzerfontein near Cape Town is a heritage and education centre that also has a museum since 2018. Together with Jos Thorne, I contributed to the section of the museum display about colonial knowledge production, which features the recordings Pöch produced in the Kalahari. See https://www.khwattu.org, accessed January 2021.

recordings. He dubbed the speaker "angry man".[262] Job Morris also informed me that |Kxara sounds very irritated. There is nothing in Pöch's summary that points to |Kxara's critique or rebuke of the Naro speakers who were present in the scene; nor can anything about their presence be drawn from Pöch's documentation. It thus remains unclear who was present, or how many people were listening to |Kxara. Even though |Kxara's speech reads like direct communication, this was not the case. As with every phonographic recording, he had to stand very close to the phonograph and speak directly into the funnel. Still, |Kxara may have used the recording situation to articulate his criticism of the Naro-speakers who were present. This seems to have happened regularly: in all collections of historical sound recordings I have studied so far, there are moments in which the recording situation became an occasion to express criticism, to articulate an appeal, or to convey a request or assessment. The addressees of these statements were by no means always the researchers.[263] The fact that speakers often have communicated with people who were listening to and watching the scene of recording, or that they may have reacted to something that was said earlier – and not necessarily by the person(s) operating or speaking into the recording device – shifts my understanding of acoustic archival collections. Practices of documentation, of archiving, together with the travelogues and reports of their expeditions that were delivered by researchers, in most cases subsequently placed the researchers, who by then had become "collectors", at the centre of the situation of the recording. This means that, following the structure of the colonial archive, we might assume that the particular researcher would also have been central in every recording situation. Yet the person who recorded may not have been of central interest to the speakers, nor were all speech acts directed at him or her as an addressee. Here it is crucial to note that the documentation of the historical sequence of recordings, which may reveal who listened and responded to whom in the course of a conversation between the speakers, may often have been corrupted by archival practices. In the archive, recordings were commonly rearranged according to the languages of the speakers or to what was assumed to be their ethnic

262   I thank all those who listened to the recordings, but especially Joram Useb who made contact with Job Morris. I also thank Kileni Fernando and Apollia Dabe in Namibia for advice and translations.
263   Hoffmann, "Finding Words (of Anger)"; "Echoes of the Great War".

background. In this way, recorded conversations became disrupted in the archive and the flow of a conversation may have become unreadable.[264]

|Kxara's triple repetition of the sentence "then you run away" appears as one audible punctum of his recording. Both his repetition of "then you run away" and the phrase "he told me he doesn't kill people" do not appear in Pöch's summaries. Fear, which Pöch had addressed derisively in his recording Ph 792, here appears as a reaction. In |Kxara's spoken text, flight appears as a strategy to escape the actual threat of the arrival of an armed white man who was well connected with the German military and with white farmers. The phrase "he told me he doesn't kill people" might explicitly name the threat that the Naro speakers saw in Pöch's arrival. Both the situation of the Naro speakers during the guerrilla war against the German colonial powers in the border zone, and Pöch's research practices, may have caused fear and horror. There were plenty of reasons to be cautious of this armed anthropologist. The phrase "that a white man is in Kxau [Kg'au tshàa], the people know" (Ph 772), uttered by a speaker named Tsuǂnoa, further indicates that the foragers who lived in the border zone, as well as Naro and Nama speakers who stayed in the vicinity of police stations or on farms, communicated through a shared network. Pöch's mention of "Bushman patrols" sent out by the police and by military to reconnoitre the area, points to channels of information that may have been used by the colonial military but may not appear in the documentation of anthropologists.[265]

Did |Kxara witness or know about exhumations that Pöch had carried out on Eduard Balzer's farm Zachas? If he knew about this practice, how did he read it? Pöch does not mention reactions or responses to his violent conduct. Yet his claim that "discontent and disputes never occurred"[266] is clearly a lie. The discord between Pöch's narrative of peaceful studies and the presence of stolen human remains that were taken to Vienna is difficult to navigate. The written records of the South African linguist Dorothea Bleek provide an adjacent source, which speaks of the

---

264 This is the case, for instance, with the recordings of Ernst and Ruth Dammann, held at the *Basler Afrika Bibliographien*. The recordings were re-arranged by the Dammanns according to languages.
265 Pöch, notebook no. 1, p. 80.
266 Pöch, "Berichte an die Akademie", 1908, p. 523; Schüller (ed.), *Rudolf Pöch's Kalahari Recordings*, p. 14.

aftermath of Pöch's research. Bleek travelled in Pöch's footsteps in 1911. On November 10 she noted: "[D]rove to Nooitgedacht [...] [W]ent on after breakfast to place of graves - found them empty, one of 5 had been removed for Pöch by Lennox".[267] Bleek's notes are undated, but she also visited the farm Zachas in 1920 and 1921 together with staff of the South African Museum. One of the aims of her trip was to excavate bodies from graves there and in Sandfontein. On the farm Zachas, where Pöch had also exhumed bodies of farm workers, and from whence a human skull had been sent to Germany by Leonhard Schultze in 1905 already, she noted the following language example[268]:

~~spook~~
the man dies
the people fetch him, take him away to the sky
only his body is buried
his life is away
he is buried
sleep well, lie
you gone one
you are buried
away the dirt, wash it off
you stay well in the grave
you are finished [in the ground?]
wash off the hands on the grave
[unnamed speaker][269]

---

267 The original can be read at: http://lloydbleekcollection.cs.uct.ac.za/books/BC_151_A3_04/A3_4_229.html, accessed January 2021. George Lennox, with whom Bleek travelled, had sent human remains to Vienna on Pöch's behalf as late as August 1910, when this was already illegal in South Africa. See Legassick and Rassool, *Skeletons in the Cupboard*, p. 28; Bank, "Anthropology and Fieldwork Photography". On Bleek's research with/on Naro speakers, see also Barnard, *Anthropology and the Bushmen*, p. 47; Weintroub, *Dorothea Bleek*.

268 Personal communication with Holger Stoecker. Leonhard Schultze was a German zoologist and anthropologist (1872-1955), see Schultze, *Aus Namaland und Kalahari: Bericht an die Kgl. Preuss. Akademie der Wissenschaften über eine Forschungsreise im westlichen u. zentralen Südafrika, ausgeführt in den Jahren 1903–1905*. Jena: Fischer, 1907.

269 http://lloydbleekcollection.cs.uct.ac.za/books/BC_151_A3_10/A3_10_004.html and http://lloydbleekcollection.cs.uct.ac.za/books/BC_151_A3_10/A3_10_005.html, accessed January 2021.

The arrangement of this text should not be read as a poem; it is a sequence of spoken example sentences, which Bleek wrote down.[270] Why she noted the word "spook" and then crossed it out, her notebook does not say. In one sense, the text reads as an account of the burial practices about which Bleek must have inquired in the course of her ethnographic study of Naro speakers and about which she writes in her book *The Naron: A Bushman Tribe of the Central Kalahari* (1928). I understand this text by the unnamed speaker as an – again very cautiously communicated – rejection of the practice of grave desecration faced by Naro speakers and other people who were classified as *Bushmen*.[271] Ten days after finding the graves already emptied by (or for) Pöch, Bleek wrote in her notebook that the people she met in the area refused to disclose burial locations: "Drove early to Sandputs, people would not tell me where to find graves".[272]

The phrases "you stay well in the grave" and "sleep well, lie" articulate a clear rejection of the practice of digging up and carrying off bodies to European and South African museums. Yet the speaker also informs Bleek about their own practices of burial, thus conveying some sense of the horror that the desecration of the graves of loved ones or ancestors must have brought for relatives, friends or descendants. The practices of grave robbery and the preparation of bodies were described by the late Martin Legassick and Ciraj Rassool two decades ago already.[273]

270 Particularly in relation to the notes of Wilhelm Bleek and Lucy Lloyd, the diction of the speakers, their repetitions, which were perhaps meant to facilitate writing them down, have often been assumed to be a poetic form and have at times been detached by interpreters from the coloniality and violence of knowledge production, see chapter 2 and Wessels, *Bushman Letters*.
271 See Legassick and Rassool, *Skeletons in the Cupboard*.
272 http://lloydbleekcollection.cs.uct.ac.za/books/BC_151_A3_04/A3_4_223.html, accessed January 2021.
273 "I heard that the white men exhumed the bodies of my husband ... my stepson and Kow's wife ... cooked their bodies in a pot and carried their bodies away. No one asked my permission to take my relatives' bodies. After I heard that the white men had taken my relatives' bodies and cooked the flesh off their bones, I prepared to leave for Langeberg to report the matter to the police, but I was told that Bushmen were outside the Law, and that I would not get a hearing. People at Kui told me this, I thought they were right and kept quiet. Since I heard that my relatives' bodies were taken and cooked, I am sick from sorrow and I will not recover from the shock for a long time. I wept for days." – "Statement of Old Katje, wife of a San exhumed by Dr Pöch's assistant", published in Legassick and Rassool, *Skeletons in the Cupboard*, p. 23 and footnote 129. The speaker describes the preparation of a body for its shipping to Vienna, which was done by Mehnarto according to Pöch's requests.

Could Pöch's joking question, "Does | Kxara think I want to devour | Kxara?" be an echo of | Kxara's possible comments, to a reaction of his, or to questions he may have asked regarding Pöch's research practices?[274] Or do we hear, in this sentence, the anthropologist responding to palpable fear in his presence? As mentioned above, I find no evidence that the speakers in general, and especially | Kxara, were afraid of the phonograph. | Kxara operated the device himself and had already spoken into the funnel by the time this wax cylinder recording was produced. | Kxara's statement, "He told me he doesn't kill people", might be a reassurance in response to the fears of those who were to be studied. | Kxara's spoken text resounds with his own position vis-à-vis the researcher, which, despite the fact that he had been subjugated to anthropometric research himself, differed from those he addressed in his recording. | Kxara told the Naro speakers, who may have tried to avoid meeting Pöch, that they need not fear for their lives. None of this appears in the written record of the recording.

An additional possibility is that both sentences ("Does | Kxara think I want to eat | Kxara?" and "He told me he doesn't kill people") can be understood as an echo of the overall violent situation of colonization, in which *foragers* had every reason to fear (armed) white men at all times. The arrival of an armed white man could have been read, for instance, in the light of frequent patrols of white farmers and/or policemen, who were in search of labourers. Marie Muschalek describes this practice as a response to a massive shortage of labour after the colonial war and genocide in Southwest Africa. During these patrols people were captured, often interrogated, and sometimes killed, their settlements were raided and destroyed, they were subsequently displaced and forced to work on farms or in houses.[275] She writes:

> On the other hand, the searches installed a general atmosphere of fear in which hiding from or disregarding the colonial labour system was less and less an option for the indigenous population.[276]

---

274 On the suspicion of cannibalism among European travellers, colonial officials and missionaries in Uganda and Congo, see Heike Behrend, *Resurrecting Cannibals: The Catholic Church, Witch-Hunts and the Production of Pagans in Western Uganda*, London: James Currey 2011, p. 155; Luise White, *Speaking with Vampires*.

275 Marie Muschalek, *Violence as Usual*, p. 137.

276 *Ibid.*, p. 140.

Fig. 19: Detail of Fig. 17.

As elsewhere, Pöch's request to speak into the phonograph had created a platform to comment on the asymmetrical power structures inherent in the research situation and beyond this immediate situation, as will be shown again in chapter 4. This means that, at times, recorded speech did preserve the speakers' response to their situation in the very moment of colonial knowledge production, the resonance of which was nevertheless lost in the archive because the researchers did not transcribe the speech acts, or transcribed them incorrectly or incompletely. Mostly these comments fell on deaf ears; they were irrelevant for the research project. Because sound recordings allow for the transmission of a different speaking position, fear can surface acoustically. Fear does not surface in the photos Pöch took of |Kxara, nor does it feature in Pöch's notes about him, yet the echo in the recording may hint at |Kxara's careful scanning of the threat posed by Pöch.

Pöch's voiced request to look after the horse, to not let it run away, becomes threatening when read in the context of the historical reality of the physical punishment of colonized people for even the smallest offences, and not only in labour relationships. These labour relationships were often based on the sheer hardship or coercion foragers experienced in the now-colonized territories. Bleek writes about the fear of the Naro speakers she interviewed:

> [...] they are dreadfully afraid of the white man, particularly the policeman, who appears to them as an arbitrary tyrant, as they do not understand the laws and never know what they may be arrested for.[277]

277 Bleek, *The Naron*, p. 42.

Bleek's description of fear ignores the actual living conditions of Naro speakers in the first decades of the 20th century. She does not mention the colonial criminalization of the foragers' way of life – for example, by means of the prohibition of hunting or the fact that mobility was criminalized as "vagrancy". Her description focuses on an alleged lack of understanding of the then-prevailing colonial law by Naro speakers. Because actual experiences of oppression and punishment do not feature in her text, fear becomes incomprehension, which she presents as an inability to understand a situation, and which thus appears irrational.

Yet the danger was real. The photograph on the following page (Fig. 20) was taken by Pöch during the so-called "camel expedition" to "Sidoni-Tsaup", which the German lieutenant Hans Kaufmann had organized for him from the Rietfontein military station. During this expedition, 262 ethnographic objects came into Pöch's possession, and he was able to examine and measure the bodies of the people he met there. Pöch does not describe the circumstances of the appropriation of the objects and the anthropometric examination in times of siege and colonial war. Here a photograph makes visible what is not told. The posturing of the two German colonial soldiers on the right, next to an arrangement of rifles, stage prevailing power relations and threatening gestures. The people squatting in the grass, who were the target group of Pöch's "visit", all look worried.[278] As already stated, it is not clear whether |Kxara the Younger was the interpreter accompanying Pöch.

Franz F. Müller's publication *Kolonien unter der Peitsche* (Colonies under the Whip) provides information on practices of corporal punishment to which people of colour were subjected in German South-West Africa. Müller describes a dramatic increase in corporal punishment and whippings in the first decade of the 20th century in the colony at that time.[279] Cane strokes were to be expected for escaping from service[280] as well as for "talking back",[281] for "indolence" and for "impertinent speech".[282] Accusations such as "talking back" or "impertinent speech" explain the tangible

---

278   This is also the case with other group and individual photos that are kept in the *Naturhistorisches Museum*, for example, and which do not appear in this book because of their racializing and objectifying presentation.
279   Franz F. Müller, *Kolonien unter der Peitsche*, Berlin: Rütten and Loening, 1962, p. 114.
280   *Ibid.*, p. 89.
281   *Ibid.*, p. 90.
282   *Ibid.*, p. 92.

Fig. 20: Camel expedition to Sidoni-Tsaup, organized by Lieutenant Hans Kaufmann.

cautiousness audible in the speech recordings, for example with regard to |Xosi Tshai's and |Kxara's comments, but also in |Xosi Tshai's sentence "I am afraid to speak" (see page 94).

Terms such as "indolence" and "impertinent speech" also demonstrate the elasticity of interpretations of misbehaviour, which left ample room for arbitrary violence against the subjugated population. Often the reason given for corporal punishment was the escape of horses or other livestock. The punishment ranged from 40 sjambok strokes meted out on a person who, "as a herder, had wandered away from cattle and thereby caused the flock to disperse", to 25 sjambok strokes suffered by a man named September "because, instead of looking after the horses, he had gone to the yard". In this context the question "*Is julle bang?*" in connection with "Did you look after the horse?" sounds threatening. In the light of the ubiquitous colonial despotism, Pöch's sentences sound like a threat communicated jokingly. The recordings Ph 792 and 763 can be heard as acoustic traces of violence as an element of colonial knowledge production as well as articulations of fear.[283]

---

283   *Ibid.*, p. 88. A sjambok/shambok is a whip made of hippopotamus or rhinoceros skin.

Fig. 21: Detail of Fig. 20.

As banal as this may sound, *close listening* here means first and foremost *listening* at all, as opposed to merely reading the documentation provided by an anthropologist who benefited from a colonial war. Only by listening can one identify Rudolf Pöch as the speaker, who was turned into a *Bushman* in the written documentation. Listening to the recordings as historical sources which resonate with moments of colonial knowledge production, alters the meaning of the acoustic documentation of the anthropologist's voice and speech. In the audio recording, | Kxara's infantilization resounds in Pöch's speech cadences and overemphasis. Job Morris's (re)translation of the acoustic recording that Pöch neither transcribed nor documented allows fear to surface for non-Naro speaking readers. This justified fear of the travelling anthropologist was trivialized and ridiculed in Pöch's speech act (and in Bleek's text some years later). It appears as very real in | Kxara's recording.

| Kxara's rebuke of the Naro-speakers remains more ambivalent. Does it resound with an act of performative distancing – feigned or not – from the position of the anthropologist's assistant vis-a-vis foragers who were the target group of Pöch's study? The acoustic recording is no less ambivalent or easier to read than | Kxara's photographs, in which he inhabits the role of the assistant behind the phonograph and in front of

Pöch's tent (Fig. 8 and Fig. 14). Although |Kxara's self-presentation is certainly one aspect of these photographs, the staging and choreography of the scene may not have reflected his choices. Despite the recurrent omissions resulting from the fragmentary quality of the sound recordings as echoes or snippets of conversation, the acoustic traces allow for a different, more multi-layered understanding of the recording situation and of the overall research context in the Ghanzi area in July and August 1908. The existence of these historical sound recordings makes it possible to return to the research situation attuned to other senses and with other archival materials, and thus with a different archival filter and under different auspices. Some of Pöch's statements and assertions turn out to be clearly false with listening. The fear of those investigated left a trace in the acoustic record; its echo speaks to the blank spaces in Pöch's writing and the documentation of what came to be known as his collection.

10607.

Alter Buschmann vom Stamme der ǃAi-khoe namens Kxara, Namelpan, Chansefeld, Britisch Betschuanaland Protektorat
(Coll. R. Pöch)

Fig. 22: |Kxara the Elder, silver gelatine print.

4 |KXARA THE ELDER RECLAIMS HIS KNIFE

On July 30 and August 13, the voice of a speaker whom Pöch called "*Ou |Kxara*" ("old |Kxara") was recorded in Kg'au tshàa[284], British Bechuanaland. In one of the recordings (Ph 771), the speaker expresses his stern critique of colonial practices of "collecting", from the perspective of someone who had formerly owned items that were appropriated to become ethnographic objects. This chapter engages with two sound recordings (🜲Ph 771 and 🜲Ph 767) and their translation by Job Morris.

According to information provided by Pöch in the protocol form, the speaker was about 50 years old when his voice was phonographed. He lived in the vicinity of the place where the recordings were produced. This speaker, whom I will call |Kxara the Elder, was photographed by Pöch at least three times. Pöch gave two of his photographs as silver gelatine prints, glued onto cardboard, to the *Naturhistorisches Museum* (Museum of Natural History) in Vienna. From there, the images migrated to the newly established *Museum für Ethnologie* (Museum of Ethnology) in Vienna in 1928, which was renamed *Weltmuseum* (World Museum) in 2017. Another photograph in which I recognize the same speaker is held in the collection of the *Department für Evolutionäre Anthropologie* (Department of Evolutionary Anthropology) at the University of Vienna, as a glass negative. In this picture, |Kxara the Elder is shown playing a mouth bow. The place and time at which the photograph was taken are not noted.

The photographs in the collection of the *Weltmuseum*, of which only one is reproduced here, show |Kxara the Elder's portrait in profile and frontal views. Together, these images form a typifying and racializing ensemble, which will not be reproduced here. The glass negative at the *Department für Evolutionäre Anthropologie* was presumably chosen to depict cultural practices of Naro speakers, whom Pöch defined and studied as *Bushmen*.[285] Unlike the two photographs (Fig. 8 and Fig. 14) published here, which stage colonial knowledge production *in situ*, and in which |Kxara

284 In Pöch's files, the place name is "Kxau".
285 See Sophie Schasiepen, "*Die Lehrmittelsammlungen*".

Fig. 23: |Kxara the Elder playing a mouth bow.

the Younger appears as Pöch's assistant, no trace of Pöch's presence appears in the photographs with |Kxara the Elder. No tent, house, or apparatus can be seen in the image; only a pile of light-coloured stones in the background, beyond the camera's focus, seems to point to human activity. Staged in an almost empty landscape which gives away nothing about the contemporaneous crisis caused by the colonial war, nor about the activity of the travelling anthropologist, |Kxara the Elder is staged as a *Bushman* playing the mouth bow.

As with the recordings with |Kxara the Younger and |Xosi Tshai, these audio, visual and textual documents, which were distributed to five separate institutions in Vienna, had not been systematically reconnected until now.[286] This means that the sound recordings with |Kxara the Elder have not been associated with the photographs held by the *Weltmuseum* on which Pöch noted his name. This particular order of things, to which all

---

286   The archivist Katarina Matiasek has been able to connect the photographs available to her (mainly from the collection at the *Department für Evolutionäre Anthropologie* at the University of Vienna) with some of Pöch's writing. Without her work, I would not have been able to find the photographs in this collection, which have not been digitized so far, as there is no catalogue and the photographs are only available there as glass negatives and prints. The photos at the *Naturhistorisches Museum* have been digitized, but most of them are not labelled, so it is difficult to assign images here as well. I would like to thank Margit Berner for the opportunity to view these photographs.

objects that Pöch had brought to Vienna were subjected by scientific and archival practices over the past 110 years, continues to direct our readings in the present. The objects' allocation to different institutions was based on disciplines and arranged around the collector's name, or around racial and ethnic denominations as principles of classification. This disciplinary order often swallowed the names of those who shared their knowledge. Traces of the speakers splintered and became fragments. The historical locations and situations of knowledge production became detached from the people who were photographed and with whom recordings were produced.

These archival practices did not merely make names and contexts disappear. They were also highly productive: foragers became nameless and placeless; objects, such as fur hats or adornments, became detached from wearers and owners; human remains of farm workers became *Bushman* remains. Many details of the connections between the objects, images, sound files and notes, which I trace and re-assemble here, may not have been available in the institutions that kept them. Connections that had once been known may have been lost or have become illegible over the years.[287] The absenting of traceable relationships between objects, places and speakers has been no more accidental than the loss of the spoken words. Instead, archival information about practices of knowledge production, and about those who had, with varying degrees of voluntarity, shared their knowledge with Pöch, disappeared systematically because the speakers, the previous owners of items, and the people whose bodies were subjected to anthropometric measurements, were of little interest to the institutions. Traces of the violent extraction processes, in the course of which tools, adornments and clothes were transformed into ethnographic objects, were obliterated by researchers, but also neglected in museums and archives. Traces of the methods that were used to create racializing images that stood (and still may stand) indexically for fabricated races and cultural entities were likewise occluded.

In the portrait (Fig. 22) and in his presentation as a mouth bow player (Fig. 23), | Kxara wears a fur hat, which, like other items of clothing depict-

---

287 This becomes clear, for instance, in the publication of Helga Maria Pacher, who does name the places where human remains have been dug up. See *Anthropologische Untersuchungen*, 1962.

ed, may have been passed between different speakers (Fig. 8) during the recording and photographic sessions.[288] The number A 157 after |Kxara's name in the recording protocol form for Ph 767 refers to the anthropometric measurements and examination of his body done by Pöch. As yet, I have not found further information on |Kxara as a person. Before Job Morris retranslated his spoken text and before the audio recordings were reconnected to the available photographs, the historical person |Kxara surfaced solely through the filter of Pöch's typification of |Kxara the Elder as *Bushman*. Pöch's representation included derogatory remarks. About recording Ph 767, Pöch states:

Zuerst spricht („Ou"-) |Kxara. Er erwähnt dass die Buschmänner so viel für mich leisten müssten (Photographie, Messungen, Phonografische Aufnahmen), und wünscht sich außer dem Tabak eine Zünddose (Feuerzeug). Tsuⱨnoa macht eine ähnliche Bemerkung und wünscht sich ein Taschenmesser. Beide Reden wurden ganz frei und ohne vorherige Proben oder Besprechung gehalten. Der alte |Kxara macht die Schnalze etwas undeutlich und gleichförmig, Tsuⱨnoa dagegen sehr gut.

("*Ou*"-) |Kxara speaks first. He mentions that the Bushmen have to do so much for me (photography, measurements, phonographic recordings), and asks for a lighter, as well as tobacco. Tsuⱨnoa makes a similar remark and asks for a pocket knife. Both recordings were spoken freely and without prior rehearsal or discussion. Old |Kxara pronounces the clicks in a somewhat

288   The *Weltmuseum* in Vienna has four of these fur hats, which, according to the list of Pöch's collection, came from Sidoni-Tsaup and were given to the collection of the museum as a gift from the *Kaiserlichen Akademie der Wissenschaften* (Imperial Academy of Sciences) in Vienna. Only one of the four hats in the museum has a similar leather rim to the hat seen in Fig. 8 and Fig. 22. For the opportunity to view the hats, the knives and other objects, I thank the curator Nadja Haumberger. Since the hats differ in style, it is conceivable that the hat worn by |Kxara the Elder and |Kxara the Younger in the photos is the same piece. Hans Kaufmann describes these fur hats, but especially hats made of the fur of the *aardwolf*, as a sign of readiness to fight or wage war, see "Die Aunin", p. 154. He describes all the men of the Aunin as "*kriegerisch und waffenfähig*" (warlike and capable of bearing arms, *ibid.*). In Kaufmann's description, their willingness to fight is presented as a racial feature. It is not seen as a reaction to danger or a crisis. Mary Louise Pratt describes this practice of representation, which naturalizes people's social strategies or their behaviour and thus situates them in an imagined ahistorical permanence, outside of historical change. Pratt provides an example: the claim that "bushmen only ever dance at night". Dancing at night thus becomes part of a naturalizing description that undercuts reactions to threat. See Pratt, *Imperial Eyes*, p. 64. In Kaufmann's case, the "warlike" attitude is naturalized and is not discussed in relation to violent colonization and guerrilla warfare.

slurred and unclear way, whereas Tsuɬnoa articulates them clearly [brackets in the original].[289]

Here, as elsewhere, the anthropologist paraphrased what was recorded as free speech and delivered his appraisal of the speaker's pronunciation of a language he neither understood nor spoke himself. In Job Morris' translation of the historical recording Ph 767, |Kxara appears as a speaker who openly expresses criticism of Pöch's behaviour:

[unclear] ... so that I don't lick my mouth and sleep like you. It is only you who is eating and I am just walking next to you ... [unclear part].
What is it with you that you eat and I am just walking beside you all? I am just like you; why are you doing this? Why are you not giving me food? Would you not also want to eat in the future? You are the only ones who are eating and I am just walking without food. Aren't we all the same people? [unclear]
Hey, white man! I'm pleading, have some remorse and give me something to lick because I'm also a human. Don't treat me like this and come closer to me. Please don't treat me like this ... [unclear]. These people are killing me, so I hope you won't kill me too because you are my friend.
[pause]
So give me a pounder to pound. You people are showing off ... why don't you give me a pounder to pound? I thought you are just a small boy? ... [unclear] ... give me something to cut [unclear] ... [does Tsuɬnoa take over speaking from here?] [290] he is giving me tobacco and cannabis to smoke ... [unclear]. Can't he make some medicine and drink? ... [unclear]

Job Morris' translation bears little resemblance to Pöch's summary. This striking dissimilarity becomes less surprising after listening to Pöch's recording of himself, which demonstrates that the anthropologist barely spoke Afrikaans and was probably unable to communicate in Naro either. The question is, what exactly did |Kxara and |Xosi Tshai choose to translate of recording Ph 767? Whether Pöch understood their translation into

289   Summary given in protocol form for recording Ph 767.
290   Tsuɬnoa is described by Pöch in the protocol form for Ph 768 as a man about 30 years of age who speaks Naro and was recorded in Kxau [Kg'au tshàa].

Afrikaans, or whether they decided not to communicate |Kxara's critique, because they sought to avoid conflict with the anthropologist, remains uncertain. Unfortunately, even after sound editing, some words and phrases remain unintelligible and are thus irretrievably lost in the noisy recording. The low quality of this historical recording also did not allow Job Morris to discern the transition between the two speakers in recording Ph 767 clearly.

What does become clear, however, is that |Kxara the Elder assumed a position to criticise the behaviour of the anthropologist, who was a guest of the group of Naro speakers for weeks but apparently did not share his food supplies with them. |Kxara's question, "Why are you not giving me food?" berates Pöch for this behaviour. His sentence, "Would you not also want to eat in the future?" presumably refers to a set of ethical agreements that form the basis of a socio-economic system of risk management, which was not based on conserving food or on savings but on symmetrical social networks. The anthropologists Polly Wiesner[291] and Alan Barnard[292] describe this system for Ju/'hoan and Naro speakers as *hxaro*:

> [...] a far reaching network of (hxaro) exchange that allowed Ju/hoansi [and, according to Barnard, Naro-speakers] to gain access to alternative residences, when food, water or social relations in the area failed. [293]

The agreement on and practice of *hxaro* entailed sharing food, water, but also access to social care, the permission to live in certain places and communal use of the resources of the land as foragers. These agreements were binding, and included inherited social practices and networks. This also means that sharing food and resources was not voluntary, nor was it based on spontaneous, individual decisions. It was obligatory. With his questions, "What is it with you that you eat and I am just walking beside you all?" and, "Aren't we all the same people?", |Kxara the Elder demanded the recognition of these obligatory practices, which presupposed an agreement on the equality of people. |Kxara the Elder articulated a clear request to

291   Polly Wiesner, "Hunting, Healing, and Hxaro Exchange: A Long-Term Perspective on
       !Kung (Ju/'hoansi) Large-Game Hunting", *Evolution and Human Behavior* 23, 2002.
292   Barnard, *Anthropology and the Bushmen*.
293   Wiesner, "Hunting, Healing, and Hxaro Exchange", p. 413; see also Barnard, *Anthropology and the Bushmen*, p. 75.

adhere to the rules of his community. He implicitly criticized the scheme of racist hierarchies within which Pöch operated. He explicitly denounced Pöch's behaviour towards Naro speakers, who had no choice but to host the uninvited guest, while the anthropologist apparently did not feel compelled to recognize or adhere to the social agreements of his hosts. Listening to the audio recordings directed my attention to several occasions where the behaviour of white settlers and travellers was addressed: | Xosi Tshai spoke of the remuneration that the farmer Taljaard claimed for "renting" him out to Pöch as an informant who could not expect to be paid himself for his services. He gave an account of forced labour practices in the colony, which Pöch profited from and obviously did not question. | Kxara the Elder pointed to obligatory social practices of sharing, to ethical agreements that applied to all who were present in communities of foragers as a crucial strategy of subsistence and survival. Pöch himself declared that he "gifted" (*"beschenkte sie mit"*) tobacco, rice and sugar to the people he examined.[294] His choice of words demonstrates that he did not consider himself obliged to follow the social rules of the people he encountered. Nor was payment for the six-hour long procedure of anthropometric measurements and photography due. In a paternalistic manner, taking advantage of asymmetrical colonial power relations, Pöch donated tobacco, sugar and worn clothes to those he subjected to anthropometric examination. | Kxara's stern criticism of Pöch's behaviour as a guest in Kg'au tshàa contradicts his own statement in his report to the Academy, that "discontent and quarrels never occurred".[295] Moreover, as in the recordings of Pöch made by himself, and with | Kxara the Younger, the topic of fear features: "I hope you won't kill me too, because you are my friend." To whom exactly the statement "These people are killing me" refers cannot be reconstructed from the recordings. Although some of the sentences spoken by | Kxara the Elder remain ambiguous, they add to what can be known of Pöch's journey and research. With the long echo of these and other acoustically preserved spoken texts, Pöch's tale of his journey loses its previous status as the only available narrative about this expedition and research, a claim which has been made repeatedly, for instance in the publication of the CD in 2003.

---

294 Pöch, "Berichte an die Akademie", 1908, p. 262.
295 *Ibid.*, p. 523.

|Kxara's second recording of free speech (Ph 771) was also retranslated by Job Morris in 2018:

[…]*ee ta I gae heea? Xgào sa máàte. Duu sa tshúù sa tsa koe? (xgoase) máàte xg'ao sa, mate xgao sa. Dtòòbès tiris koe ra tcaa si kg'oana haa ke. máàte xg'ao sa, thuu ra cgóbè tsi si hãa igaba tsi thuu ta kãbi, ta hẽe te na kar nc̃ẽe ta nòòse kg'ui guu. Duu sa tshúù sa tsa koe? Tcaoa x'aèan tsi thuu xgàos sa uua hãa. Xgào sa kãbi máàte. Máàte tiris xgao sa. Wêê ne ga ko tsa ka koase hãase kg'ui igaba tsi duus ka tiris xgào sa máàte tama, atsee? Ncee camka, nc̃ẽem cam ka tsi gha tiri xgào sa máàte. Nãi ser thuu biri tsi a màà tiris xgào sa máàte temea tsi thuu maa" ee" teme ra thuu kom tsia hãa, nxa kg'aiga a, thuu ra dtòòbès koe xgào sa tcaa kg'oana. Gaea qam se naka x'oo tama. Thuu tsi xgao sa nc̃ẽe thuu qaem nxoem ka sèè me nc̃ẽeska thuu gam nxoe ba x'oo igaba tsi qanega tiris xgao sa kãbi máàte tama. Gam khama tsi ga ko maa dqari igaba tsi gha se ne xgào sa máàte, ga tama ko ii ne tsi nceem cam ka xom tite.*

[record starts with static and unclear voices] What's wrong with you? Give me the knife. What's wrong with you? [getting angry at this point] Give me the knife, give me the knife. I want to put it in my bag. Give me the knife. Give me the knife, I lent it to you and you never gave it back. Don't let me talk this much. What's wrong with you? You kept the knife long enough. Give me the knife back. Give me my knife... [long pause] ... They are all talking about you boastingly but why are you not giving me my knife, hey? This day ... today, you will give me back my knife. I told you long time ago to give me my knife and you said "yes" and I heard you ... Since then, I wanted to put the knife in the bag. […] You took a knife last moon and now it has died [last moon = last month, A.H.] but you haven't given me my knife back yet. Even if you sound like a lion, you should give me the knife, because today you will not sleep keeping my knife ... [record ends with unclear voice].

As a reason for a second recording with |Kxara the Elder, Pöch mentioned technical problems with the previous recording. Again, his main concern was the acoustic preservation of the sound of words and the melody of the pronunciation. Like |Kxara the Younger and |Xosi Tshai, |Kxara the Elder used the opportunity of recording to air critique. Both his recordings are listed as free speech. This means that what he said was not rehearsed or agreed upon beforehand, as had been the case with some of the other language examples recorded. Pöch summarizes the content of the recording as follows:

Bermerkungen zum Inhalt der Rede:
| Kxara sagt, er habe für seine früheren Leistungen sehr rasch ein Messer erhalten, nun dauert es so lange, bis er die versprochene Feuerdose bekommt, er möchte sie endlich haben (| Kxara bekam seine Feuerdose)
Notes on the content of the speech:
| Kxara says he received a knife very quickly for his previous services, now it is taking so long for him to get the promised fire box, he wants it at last (| Kxara got his fire box).

[Bracket in the original]

Again, it remains uncertain how this summary, which does not correspond with Job Morris' transcription and translation, came about. The question of who understood whom, who understood what, and whose interpretation actually appeared in the booklet that came with the CD, is therefore hard to assess.

Of all the historical recordings discussed in this book, the recordings with | Kxara the Elder most directly air discontent with the anthropologist's behaviour. As with | Xosi Tshai's account of his unpaid labour for Pöch, the anthropologist apparently felt compelled to comment on the recording. Perhaps | Kxara's anger was audible, even though his words were not translated. | Kxara's bold statements can be heard as an echo of his enunciative position: unlike | Xosi Tshai and | Kxara the Younger, he did not work for Pöch. He thus did not speak from a position of dependency. | Kxara seems unfazed by the consequences that his critique of Pöch's conduct could have had for him. An additional reason for this could have been that he was well aware that the anthropologist was not able to understand him, unless his words were translated by Pöch's assistants. | Kxara's last two sentences of recording Ph 771 sound especially like a threat: "Even if you sound like a lion, you should give me the knife, because today you will not sleep keeping my knife..." | Kxara the Elder repeated this explicit reclaiming of his knife *eight times*. His recording resounds with the anger of a man who demands the return of a tool, which may have been vital to him and which Pöch had probably taken, under circumstances that cannot be reconstructed.

Clearly, for a group of people who lived as foragers, who most likely called very few material possessions their own, and whose lives were under threat in times of war and drought, knives were essential tools. Moreover, they must have been particularly difficult to replace during this period. The knives were not produced by the foragers themselves; they were objects of trade. The few knives that Pöch got hold of in Sidoni-Tsaup, together with dozens of bracelets and pieces of beadwork, are now kept by the *Weltmuseum* in Vienna. About a knife with the inventory number 85658, which came into his possession during the so-called camel expedition to Sidoni-Tsaup, Pöch writes:

> *Messer „Kxai" mit Eisenklinge, schmal-lanzettliche Klinge [...] die in den Holzgriff eingelassen ist [...] Der Holzgriff ist stark beschädigt, Ovambo Arbeit.*
>
> Knife "Kxai" with narrow-lanced iron blade [...] set into wooden handle [...] The wooden handle is damaged, made by Ovambo [*Ovambo Arbeit*].

This knife, like the others from the Kalahari, is an object that had previously been in use when it came into Pöch's possession. Before these items were turned into ethnographic objects, they were among the personal belongings of people whom we do not get to know by name.

In the transcriptions of the audio recordings produced by Dorothea Bleek in Namibia in 1911, I found spoken accounts of Naro speakers, who discuss trading and bartering leather garments for knives. The first speaker begins her account with the announcement, "Of goods I speak", which, according to Dorothea Bleek, she repeated five times.[296] This is followed by two very detailed descriptions of who traded what with whom, recorded with a Naro speaker, an "Auen" (Ju/'hoan?) speaker, and her husband. Bleek translated the spoken texts as follows:

> You Naron sell aprons, we exchange goods with you; Auen beads, we give beads. That is the custom, we people exchange with people. That is the custom, we people give knives. We give knives - it is finished.[297]

296 Transcription from Dorothea Bleek, *Gramophone Records*, Special Collections, University of Cape Town, Folder *E 5.1.17-E 5*, notes on the sound recordings made by Bleek with a Lieutenant Jordaan, which are undated. I assume they date from 1911. The names of the speakers do not appear in the transcriptions. I thank Digital Library Services and especially Niklas Zimmer for the digitization.

297 Extract from transcriptions to Record III, D. Bleek, *BL 151 E 5.1.18*, Special Collections, University of Cape Town. The phrase, "It is finished", refers to the end of her speech.

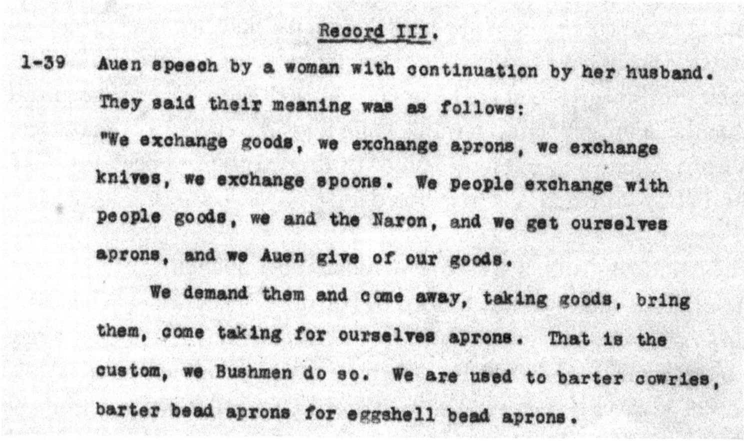

Record III.

1-39 Auen speech by a woman with continuation by her husband.
They said their meaning was as follows:

"We exchange goods, we exchange aprons, we exchange
knives, we exchange spoons. We people exchange with
people goods, we and the Naron, and we get ourselves
aprons, and we Auen give of our goods.

We demand them and come away, taking goods, bring
them, come taking for ourselves aprons. That is the
custom, we Bushmen do so. We are used to barter cowries,
barter bead aprons for eggshell bead aprons.

*Fig. 24: Excerpt from transcriptions of Dorothea Bleek's notes on her sound recordings, undated, proba-
bly October 1911.[298]*

The phrase, "you Naron sell aprons," refers to garments made of leather
for barter, for example for knives.[299]

Robert Gordon mentions knives as objects of trade, mostly import-
ed from the northern regions of Namibia and exchanged for ostrich egg
beads, animal skins, or garments made of leather.[300] In times of drought,
of siege, and of war, when game was scarce and freedom of movement
was restricted, many foragers would ensure that they stayed close to boreholes. The prohibition of hunting by the German colonial power, the
implementation of restrictions of movement that were caused by war
and intensified border controls between South West Africa and British
Bechuanaland endangered the survival of foragers in the region. Getting

---

298 The previous recording refers to dances and corresponds with her notebook no. 5, p.
336, available at "Digital Bleek and Lloyd" http://lloydbleekcollection.cs.uct.ac.za/in-
dex.html, accessed January 2021.

299 It seems to me that trade has long been under-represented in researchers' descriptions
of the ways of life of the people referred to as *Bushmen* (see also Gordon, *The Bushman
Myth*). Interestingly, although the beginning of this recording ("of trade we speak") appears as an example of language in Bleek's book *The Naron* (1928), Bleek did not devote
a chapter to trade, which was obviously important to the speaker. The chapters are divid-
ed into topics such as "Modes of Life", "Fire and Food", "Paint and Tattoo", "Weapons",
"Hunting and Trapping" or "Games".

300 Gordon, *The Bushman Myth*, pp. 26–28.

hold of ostrich eggs to make beads or animal skins for trading had become increasingly difficult. As a result, knives must have been indispensable. Revisiting | Kxara the Elder's urgent, very angry, reiterated demand that the anthropologist return his knife leads directly to the *Weltmuseum* Vienna, where the greatest proportion of the objects that Pöch carried off from the Kalahari to Austria is stored today.

THE APPROPRIATION OF OBJECTS WITH MILITARY SUPPORT

The bulk of the 1061 objects listed by Barbara Plankensteiner in her essay on Pöch's collection came from Oas and from Sidoni-Tsaup. Only a few objects came from Kg'au tshàa, where Pöch pitched his tent from 10 July to 7 September 1908.[301] In Oas, Pöch boarded at a military station from 30 January to 29 April of 1908. He travelled to Sidoni-Tsaup, where he stayed for only two days, from 6 to 8 June in 1908, with the so-called "camel expedition" organized especially for him by the *Schutztruppe's* border station in Rietfontein (Fig. 19).

According to Plankensteiner it remains unclear whether Pöch was as ruthless about acquiring ethnographica as he was about "collecting human remains".[302] She also points to a significant distinction in the way Pöch registered objects acquired in the museum's inventory book: all objects that were related to *Bushmen* were registered as "*Aufsammlungen*". *Aufsammeln* (as a verb) in German translates as "picking" or "picking up", which designates practices of acquisition that do not entail barter or payment, or indeed any human interaction at all. Objects that related to other ethnic groups were registered by Pöch as "*Ankäufe*" (purchases).[303] By this differentiation, Pöch implicitly placed so-called *Bushman* objects, to which Plankensteiner refers as "San ethnographica", into a different time frame from other items, for instance, those he had acquired from Otjiherero

301 Plankensteiner, "Auch hier gilt die Regel", p. 97.
302 Regarding practices of "collecting human remains", she refers to the publication by Legassick and Rassool, *Skeletons in the Cupboard*. Because Pöch himself did not publish on the objects he brought from southern Africa, she reads the collection together with the texts of Walter Hirschberg (1904-1996), which the latter submitted as a professorial dissertation with the title *Völkerkundliche Ergebnisse der südafrikanischen Reisen Rudolf Pöch's in den Jahren 1907 bis 1909*. See Plankensteiner, "Auch hier gilt die Regel", p. 95. At the time of the article's publication, Barbara Plankensteiner was the head of the "Africa South of the Sahara" collection at the *Museum für Völkerkunde* in Vienna (now the *Weltmuseum*).
303 Plankensteiner, "Auch hier gilt die Regel", p. 101.

speakers. In accordance with the understanding of *Bushmen* as remnants of the past, acquiring their belongings thus appears as an archaeological practice. Apart from this, Plankensteiner contends that Pöch's statements do not allow further conclusions about the practices of acquisition to be drawn.[304] The Austrian anthropologist Walter Hirschberg, who discussed Pöch's collection from the Kalahari in a 1936 essay, states that plates of to-bacco, lighters, matches, pocket knives, worn clothes or blankets were used as payment for the objects that the anthropologist brought to Vienna. Hirschberg does not disclose the source for this statement.[305] It is possible that all of Pöch's notebooks were still available in 1936.

Plankensteiner's statement, that no further conclusions can be drawn on the appropriation of objects, becomes questionable after listening to the recordings. Clearly, very little can be learned about the methods of extractive knowledge production and appropriation if we, as researchers of provenance in the present, expect truthful reports from so-called collectors. As long as the statements of grave robbers, academic profiteers of colonial wars, and thieves are considered the most reliable or even the only available sources for provenance research, we will not leave colonial epistemic paradigms. In other words, we will not be able to include the positions of those whose tools, belongings, artworks, or documents have been captured if we continue to rely on documentation provided by those who brought the spoils of their expeditions to Europe.

As far as Pöch's research is concerned, I would like to repeat that the appropriation of objects in the Kalahari on a grand scale (which only subsequently became "ethnographica" or "*Bushman* objects"), took place during a colonial war. Gesa Grimme's detailed provenance research at the *Lindenmuseum* in Stuttgart shows that the volume of the ethnographic holdings from Namibia increased exponentially during and immediately after the colonial war in this country.[306] The war in South West Africa pro-vided "opportunities" for looting deserted homes after battles, and for robbing the dead of their belongings. German soldiers and colonial ad-ministrators were also able to capture artworks and religious artefacts un-der conditions of war, terror, and flight. The human remains of victims of

304   *Ibid.*
305   Hirschberg, *Völkerkundliche Ergebnisse der südafrikanischen Reisen*, p. 1.
306   Grimme, "Annäherung an ein schwieriges Erbe"; for museums in France see Sarr and Savoy, "Zurückgeben".

the war were regularly carried off and given or sold to German museums and research institutions. On some of Pöch's photographs in the *Weltmuseum*, the caption "scattered Herero" (*verstreute Herero*) appears. He does not note whether the people he photographed had fled from German South West Africa to British Bechuanaland (Botswana) during the genocidal war in South West Africa.

In the context of the power relations during this war and the gaps in the narratives of appropriation-as-"collecting", the massive numbers of objects that Pöch was able to get hold of reveal his strategies of extraction. While Pöch was living at the military station in Oas, he brought 138 objects from people he called *Bushmen* into his possession; during the far briefer camel expedition to Sidoni-Tsaup, he was able to appropriate 262 objects. The register of the *Weltmuseum* in Vienna also shows that from Kg'au tshàa, where Pöch stayed without a military escort, only 19 objects entered his collection. Presumably, without military support, that is, without the threatening presence of colonial soldiers, and outside the centres of colonial power, such as the station in Rietfontein, Pöch could not easily get hold of the possessions of Naro speakers. Nor could he force them into asymmetrical barter deals. The recording in which | Kxara the Elder vehemently demands his knife back resounds as a moment of resistance against Pöch's practices of appropriation. There may have been other incidents, yet these do not appear in Pöch's narrative of his expedition.

The list of objects, which was written by the anthropologist, does not tell whether around 100 poison arrows, many bags, four tobacco pouches, four other pouches, four fur hats, one pair of sandals, 160 bracelets, two knives, many hair ornaments, one of which was cut off with some of the hair of its owner, together with head ornaments, necklaces, lighters, and other objects, had changed hands under threat in Sidoni-Tsaup. Perhaps some of these items were indeed for sale. A photograph Pöch took during the so-called camel expedition depicts white soldiers posing next to an array of rifles (Fig. 25).

In terms of what can be known about colonial practices of amassing items – for instance in southern Africa – which would become ethnographic objects in museums in Europe, the audio recording with | Kxara the Elder may be a game changer. To my knowledge, this is the only acoustically archived statement on violent expropriation uttered by a former owner of one of the tools, adornments, and perhaps objects of trade that

Fig. 25: Detail from Fig. 20, camel expedition to Sidoni-Tsaup.

have been part of the museum collection in Vienna for 110 years now. And although this is the only audio recording that I know of in which a person who was subjected to racializing studies resisted the appropriation of his belongings, I believe that a more systematic study of historical audio recordings of the colonial archive would unearth more such statements.

LISTENING TO THE COLONIAL ARCHIVE

The search for |Kxara's knife sends me to the depot of the *Weltmuseum* in Vienna. Here, dimmed lights and regulated temperatures are intended to protect ethnographic objects. Neatly lined up, separated from their previous owners, detached from their former uses, but also from the violent practices of their procurement, the objects seem to doze on the shelves. Before I am allowed to enter the storage rooms in the basement of the *Weltmuseum*, I have to slip on a white coat. The curator's rubber-gloved hands carefully place the knives I have asked to see on a table, which is covered with white foil. Fur hats, now partly bald, and beaded jewellery, still red with Kalahari dust, are handled just as carefully. The curatorial care extended to these items after they were numbered, labelled, and classified, contrasts sharply with the violence of their acquisition during a brutal colonial war. 160 similar bracelets from Sidoni-Tsaup tell of Rudolf Pöch's greed and his drive for recognition. More than 100 years ago, these objects

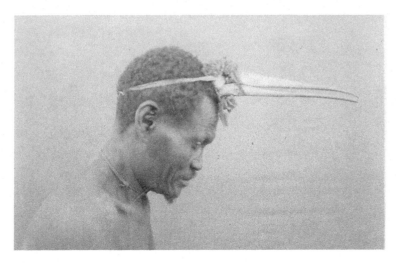

Fig. 26: Man with bird mask, detail, Oas, 1908.

became the capital with which Pöch built his career as an anthropologist.[307] With few exceptions, the former owners of items do not feature in the museum's inventory books.

Little is left of the beauty and magic of a bird mask, once photographed with its wearer, whose name Pöch noted as "Damab". Discoloured and robbed of its performative power, in the repository in Vienna it has become the faint shadow of a mask that perhaps once enabled its wearer to become a startling birdman. Now the discoloured remains of a skull and a beak communicate the immense sadness of *chosification*, the "thingification" which Aimé Césaire placed at the heart of colonial knowledge production.[308]

Like most objects from the Kalahari, this bird mask probably never left the storerooms of the museum. Like the mask, which *chosification* turned into the remains of a dead bird in the repository, the sound recordings from the Kalahari have changed in the archive. Detached from their performative meaning, from speakers, from the context of their production, they have become fragmented echoes of speech acts and

307   Sophie Schasiepen, *Southern African Human Remains as Property: Physical Anthropology and the Production of Racial Capital in Austria,* Ph.D., Department of History, University of the Western Cape, South Africa, 2021.
308   Aimé Césaire, *Über den Kolonialismus.*

songs performed more than hundred years ago. The capacity of extractive knowledge production to swallow spoken words has silenced the speaker's critique for decades; it is irreconcilably opposed to the curatorial care of preserving the sound recordings as objects.

We did not find |Kxara's knife in the museum repository. Perhaps |Kxara was able to exact its return. Yet, while his knife may not have become part of Pöch's spoils, the recording with |Kxara the Elder, once listened to again, continues to criticize colonial practices of appropriation. His recorded words echo a speaking position which had no place in the written or visual documentation of Pöch's expedition. Job Morris's translation allowed |Kxara to shed the role of the "loquacious speaker" assigned to him by the anthropologist. Instead, he appears as a resolute critic of colonial violence. By means of close listening, translation, and the reconnection of the recordings with photographs, texts and objects, |Kxara's words have regained their ability to speak. Most importantly, |Kxara's unflinching critique of colonial research and his rejection of the appropriation of his belongings testify that protest was already being voiced in 1908.

Translation, close listening, and the work of reassembling a collection places |Kxara's spoken texts in the company of other critical recordings from collections of historical sound recordings: a recording that speaks of the destruction of a sacred shrine in Ghana (Stephan Bischoff, Berlin 1916, *Lautarchiv* Berlin), a recording that criticizes the making of life casts of people for the purpose of racial research (Wilfred Tjiueza, Namibia 1931, *Phonogramm-Archiv* Berlin), a recording that asks where these casts will be taken and who will look at them (Kanaje, Namibia 1931, *Phonogramm-Archiv* Berlin), a recording that speaks of the colonial war as the cause of the irreversible loss of social cohesion (Adelheid Mbwaondjou, Namibia 1954, *Basler Afrika Bibliographien*).[309]

309 For Kanaje's and Wilfred Tjiueza's recordings, see Hoffmann "Finding Words (of Anger)"; for Adelheid Mbwaondjou's recordings, see my sound/text installation "*Die Kette*", of 2019 at the Lindenmuseum Stuttgart; for the recordings of the Dammann collection see Julia Rensing, Lorena Rizzo and Wanda Rutishauser (eds.), *Sites of Contestation: Encounters with the Ernst and Ruth Dammann Collection in the Archives of the Basler Afrika Bibliographien*, 2021, Basel: Basler Afrika Bibliographien; Heike Becker,"'Let me come to tell you': Loide Shikongo, the King, and Poetic License in Colonial Ovamboland", *History and Anthropology* 16 (2), 2005, 235-258, and Nashilongweshipwe Mushaandja's sonic engagement with these recordings, https://soundcloud.com/tschukutschuku.

These audio recordings do not offer the only texts of contemporary witnesses to colonial knowledge production, as the linguist Dorothea Bleek's language examples show. The occasion of acoustic recording, but more generally the invitation "to speak", provided the opportunity to give an account of the colonial present, or to communicate concern and disagreement. Yet there is a clear difference between, for instance, reading Bleek's transcriptions and translations, versus collaborative listening and reading an informed retranslation of the recordings that were made with the two |Kxaras and with |Xosi Tshai. Although historical sound recordings should not be understood as unmediated "voices from the past", they can and do transmit an audible echo of speakers' statements, and thus an echo of colonial knowledge production. In felicitous cases, well-preserved recordings still transmit the performativity and melody of a speaker's voice, the rhythm of speech, and sometimes even the sound of the speakers' breath. In some instances, even the presence of an audience is audible. Together with linguists' or anthropologists' transcriptions, acoustic recordings make it possible to hear the dissonance between speakers, who spoke in order to communicate, and researchers, who recorded and heard examples of speech.

To date, collections of historical sound recordings have often been subjected to similar practices of curatorial care as the ethnographic objects in museum. Recordings on wax cylinders, in particular, have long been regarded as *incunabula,* the precious, irreplaceable artefacts which testify to the history of sound recording. They have very rarely been heard or treated as potential sources of colonial history. In the order of things hitherto assigned to them, the straitjacket of the colonial archive, their reduction to objects for linguistics or musicology, and their durable archival isolation from speakers, speaking situations, repertoires, and genres, they have become ossified and fallen silent. Paradoxically, archiving was able to preserve as well as to silence spoken statements. Practices of acquisition, along with persisting colonial epistemes and disciplinary seclusion, have swallowed their historical content. In the colonial archive, historical sound recordings have been barely distinguishable from the other fetishized objects in ethnological collections. Not unlike the bird's beak or the hundreds of bracelets from the Kalahari, their former performative meaning, their ability to speak of colonial violence, has long been dormant.

In the written documentation published together with the sound recordings from the Kalahari, the brutality of the capture of objects, the fear and anger of the speakers, and the epistemic violence of Pöch's research do not feature. Nor does the gibberish of the Austrian anthropologist, which he recorded himself, appear in the CD's list of items.

In order to reactivate historical sound recordings, they need to be wrested from the disciplinary order that has muted them, and that continues to keep them silent. The recordings must be reconnected to other traces their speakers left in the archive, to the historical situations of knowledge production, and to colonial practices of research, which informed their making. Historical recordings must leave the archive to be discussed with or by speakers of the languages in which they were recorded so as to become meaningful documents of colonial history. The recordings from the Kalahari which appear in this book show that it is worthwhile to undertake this work systematically: sound recordings are acoustic sources of colonial history. They may contain positions of speakers that do not surface elsewhere, and they resound with the history of chauvinistic, often violent, knowledge production. They speak of practices of appropriation and of the permanent and systematic elision of these practices in European archives. They testify to the durability of the misappropriation of the speakers' role in colonial knowledge production.

If we include historical sound recordings in our understanding of the colonial archive, the presence or absence of subaltern speaking positions in the colonial archive will have to be discussed again, this time on the basis of thousands of speech acts, texts and songs not previously heard as statements outside of their disciplines. When historical sound recordings are understood as part of the colonial archive, the archive speaks in many voices.

LIST OF THE SOUND RECORDINGS DISCUSSED

Recorded by Rudolf Pöch, 1908, Phonogrammarchiv Vienna, in the order of their appearance in the text.

Ph 789: Kubi, 22 August 1908, Kg'au tshàa British Bechuanaland (modern Botswana) – this is the scratched record, soundtrack of the film *Buschmann spricht in den Phonographen.*
🔊 https://www.austriaca.at/audio/Serie7-Kalahari/18_Ph789.mp3

Ph 785: Kubi, barely translatable, 22 August 1908, Kg'au tshàa, British Bechuanaland (modern Botswana), edited by Job Morris, 2018.
🔊 https://www.austriaca.at/audio/Serie7-Kalahari/14_Ph785.mp3

Ph 786: |Xosi Tshai, 23 August 1908, Kg'au tshàa British, Bechuanaland (present-day Botswana), not retranslated.
🔊 https://www.austriaca.at/audio/Serie7-Kalahari/15_Ph786.mp3

Ph 781: |Xosi Tshai, 22 August 1908, Kg'au tshàa, British Bechuanaland (modern Botswana), retranslated by Job Morris, 2018.
🔊 https://www.austriaca.at/audio/Serie7-Kalahari/12_Ph781.mp3

Ph 792: Rudolf Pöch, undated, 1908, Kg'au tshàa, British Bechuanaland (present-day Botswana).
🔊 https://www.austriaca.at/audio/Serie7-Kalahari/20_Ph792.mp3

Ph 763: |Kxara the Younger, 27 July 1908, Kg'au tshàa, British Bechuanaland (modern Botswana), retranslated by Job Morris, 2018.
🔊 https://www.austriaca.at/audio/Serie7-Kalahari/1_Ph763.mp3

Ph 767: |Kxara the Elder and Tsuǂnoa, 30 July 1908, Kg'au tshàa, British Bechuanaland (present-day Botswana), retranslated by Job Morris, 2018.
🔊 https://www.austriaca.at/audio/Serie7-Kalahari/2_Ph767.mp3

Ph 771: |Kxara the Elder, 13 August 1908, Kg'au tshàa, British Bechuanaland (present-day Botswana), retranslated by Job Morris, 2018.
🔊 https://www.austriaca.at/audio/Serie7-Kalahari/6_Ph771.mp3

GLOSSARY OF CHARACTERS APPEARING IN THE TEXT FOR CLICK SOUNDS IN NARO

Click sounds are consonants that occur in many South African languages.

ǀ is a dental click that is written c for some languages.

ǂ is a palatal click written ç (tc, qc) for some languages.

! is an alveolar click written q for some languages.

ǁ is a lateral click written x for some languages.

It is not clear whether Pöch spelled the clicks correctly. For names and places that I take from Pöch, I use the spelling he used.

LIST OF ILLUSTRATIONS

Fig. 17, p. 117: Military station Rietfontein, photographed by Rudolf Pöch, 1908, *Naturhistorisches Museum*, Vienna.

Fig. 18, p. 119: Portrait of | Kxara, photographed by Rudolf Pöch, 1908, *Department für Evolutionäre Anthropologie*, University of Vienna.

Fig. 19, p. 126: Detail from Fig. 17, photographed by Rudolf Pöch, 1908, *Naturhistorisches Museum*, Vienna.

Fig. 20, p. 128: Military expedition to Sidoni-Tsaup, photographed by Rudolf Pöch, 1908, *Department für Evolutionäre Anthropologie*, University of Vienna.

Fig. 21, p. 129: Detail from Fig. 20.

Fig. 22, p. 132: | Kxara the Elder, photographed by Rudolf Pöch, 1908, *Weltmuseum*, Vienna.

Fig. 23, p. 134: | Kxara the Elder, photographed by Rudolf Pöch, 1908, *Department für Evolutionäre Anthropologie*, University of Vienna.

Fig. 24, p. 143: Extract from Dorothea Bleek's notes on her sound recordings, probably 1911, Special Collections, University of Cape Town.

Fig. 25, p. 147: Detail from Fig. 20.

Fig. 26, p. 148: Man with bird mask, detail, photographed by Rudolf Pöch, Oas, 1908, *Weltmuseum*, Vienna.

BIBLIOGRAPHY

Adhikari, Mohamed, *The Anatomy of a South African Genocide: The Extermination of the Cape San Peoples*, Cape Town: University of Cape Town Press, 2010.

Ankermann, Bernhard, *Anleitung zum ethnographischen Beobachten und Sammeln*, Berlin: Georg Reimer Verlag, 1914.

Bam, June, "Contemporary Khoisan Heritage Issues in South Africa: A Brief Historical Overview", Lungisile Ntsebeza and Chris Saunders (eds.), *Papers from the Pre-Colonial Catalytic Project, Vol. 1*, Cape Town: University of Cape Town Press 2014, 123–133.

Bam, June, *Ausi Told Me: Why Cape Herstoriographies Matter*, Johannesburg: Fanele and Jacana Media, 2021.

Bank, Andrew, "Anthropology and Fieldwork Photography: Dorothea Bleek's Expedition to the Northern Cape and the Kalahari, July to December 1911", *Kronos* 32, 2006, 77–113.

Bank, Andrew, *Bushmen in a Victorian World: The Remarkable Story of the Bleek-Lloyd Collection of Bushman Folklore*, Cape Town: Double Storey Books, 2006.

Barnard, Alan, *Anthropology and the Bushmen*, Oxford and New York: Berg, 2007.

Becker, Heike "'Let me come to tell you': Loide Shikongo, the King, and Poetic License in Colonial Ovamboland", *History and Anthropology* 16 (2), 2005, 235-258.

Behrend, Heike, "Ham Mukasa wundert sich: Bemerkungen zur Englandreise eines Afrikaners (1902)", Heike Behrend and Thomas Geider (eds.), *Afrikaner schreiben zurück: Texte und Bilder afrikanischer Ethnographen*, Cologne: Köppe Verlag 1998, 323–338.

Behrend, Heike, *Resurrecting Cannibals: The Catholic Church, Witch-Hunts and the Production of Pagans in Western Uganda*, London: James Currey, 2011.

Biesele, Megan, *Women Like Meat: The Folklore and Foraging Ideology of Kalahari Ju/'hoan*, Johannesburg: Wits University Press, 1993.

Birdsall, Carolyn, *Nazi Soundscapes: Sound, Technology and Urban Space in Germany, 1933-1945*, Amsterdam: University of Amsterdam Press, 2012.

Bleek, Dorothea F., *The Naron: A Bushman Tribe of the Central Kalahari*, London: Cambridge University Press, 1928.

Bleek, Wilhelm Heinrich Immanuel, *Über den Ursprung der Sprache*, Weimar: Böhlau, 1868.

Bleek, Wilhelm Heinrich Immanuel, *Reineke Fuchs in Afrika: Fabeln und Märchen der Eingeborenen, Nach Original Handschriften der Grey'schen Bibliothek und anderen authentischen Quellen.* Weimar: Böhlau, 1870.

Blommaert, Jan, "Artefactual Ideologies and the Textual Production of African Languages", *Language and Communication* 28, 2008, 291–307.

Brady, Erika, *A Spiral Way: How the Phonograph Changed Ethnography*, Jackson: MS Press, 1999.

Brenzinger, Matthias, "Classifying Non-Bantu Click Languages", Lungisile Ntsebeza and Chris Saunders (eds.), *Papers from the Pre-Colonial Catalytic Project, Vol. 1*, Cape Town: University of Cape Town Press 2014, 80–102.

Cavero, Adriana, "For More Than One Voice", Thomas Trummer (ed.), *Voice and Void*, New York: The Aldrich Contemporary Art Museum, 2007, 44–57.

Césaire, Aimé, *Über den Kolonialismus*. Aus dem Französischen, mit einer Vorbemerkung und Anmerkungen von Heribert Becker, Berlin: Alexander Verlag, 2017.

Challis, Sam, "Retribe and Resist: The Deliberate Ethnogenesis of a Creolised Raiding Band in Response to Colonisation", Carolyn Hamilton and Nessa Leibhammer (eds.), *Tribing and Untribing the Archive*, Vol. 1, Pietermaritzburg: University of KZN Press 2017, 283–307.

Chatterjee, Partha, "After Subaltern Studies", *Economic and Political Weekly* XLVII (35), 2012, 44–49.

Chidester, David, "Mutilating Meaning: European Interpretations of Khoisan Languages of the Body", Pippa Skotnes (ed.) *Miscast: Negotiating the Presence of the Bushmen*, Cape Town: University of Cape Town Press 1996, 21-41.

Deumert, Ana, *Variation and Standardisation: The Case of Afrikaans (1880–1922)*, Cape Town: University of Cape Town Press, 1999.

Dieckmann, Ute, *Hai//om in the Etoscha Region*, Basel: Basler Afrika Bibliographien, 2007.

Doegen, Wilhelm, *Unsere Gegner damals und heute: Engländer und Franzosen und ihre fremdrassigen Hilfsvölker in der Heimat, an der Front und in Gefangenschaft im Weltkriege und im jetzigen Kriege, Großdeutschlands koloniale Sendung*, Berlin 1941.

Dolar, Mladen, *A Voice and Nothing More*, Cambridge, Massachusetts, and London: MIT Press, 2006.

Dubow, Saul, *Scientific Racism in Modern South Africa*, Cambridge: The University of Cambridge Press, 1995.

Du Plessis, Menán, "The Damaging Effects of Romantic Mythopoeia on Khoesan Linguistics", *Critical Arts* 28 (3), 2014, 569–592.

Ebeling, Knut, and Stephan Günzel, *Archivologie: Theorien des Archivs in Philosophie, Medien und Künsten*, Berlin: Kadmos, 2009.

Edwards, Elizabeth, *Raw Histories: Photographs, Anthropology and Museums*, Oxford: Oxford University Press, 2001.

Foroutan, Naika, *et al.* (eds.) *Das Phantom "Rasse": Zur Geschichte und Wirkungsmacht von Rassismus*, Cologne: Böhlau, 2018.

Foucault, Michel, *Power, Truth, Strategy*, Working Papers No. 2, edited by Meghan Morris and Paul Patton, Sidney: Feral Publications, 1979.

Foucault, Michel, *Archäologie des Wissens*, Frankfurt am Main: Suhrkamp, 1981.

Franzen, Jannik, *Bilder der „Anderen", geformt am Schillerplatz: Rassistische Forschungen an Kriegsgefangenen im Ersten Weltkrieg und die Akademie der bildenden Künste Wien*, unpublished MA thesis, Academy of Fine Arts Vienna, 2019.

Fritsch, Gustav, "Die Buschmänner der Kalahari von S. Passarge", *Zeitschrift für Ethnologie* 38 (1/2), 1906, 71–79.

Fuhrmann, Wolfgang, "Ethnographic Films from Prisoner-of-War Camps and the Aesthetics of Early Cinema", Reinhard Johler, Christian Marchetti and Moniqua Scheer (eds.), *Doing Anthropology in Wartime and War Zones: World War I and the Cultural Sciences in Europe*, Bielefeld: Transcript 2010, 337–352.

Garbe, Sebastian, "Das Projekt Modernität/Kolonialität: Zum theoretischen/akademischen Umfeld des Konzepts der Kolonialität der Macht", Sebastian Garbe and Pablo Qintero (eds.), *Kolonialität der Macht: De/Koloniale Konflikte zwischen Theorie und Praxis*, Münster: Unrast Verlag 2013, 21–46.

García, Miguel A., "Sound Archives under Suspicion", Susanne Ziegler, Ingrid Åkesson, Gerda Lechleitner and Susana Gardo (eds.), *Histori-*

cal Sources of Ethnomusicology in Contemporary Debate, Cambridge: Cambridge Scholars, 2017.

Gehrmann, Petra, "Die Wiederholungsstimme: Über die Strafe der Echo", Doris Kolesch and Sybille Krämer (eds.), *Stimme*, Frankfurt am Main: Suhrkamp 2006, 85–111.

Gilroy, Paul, *Against Race: Imagining Political Culture Beyond the Color Line*, Cambridge, Massachusetts: Belknap Press and Harvard University Press, 2000.

Glen, Ian, "The Bushman in Early South African Literature", Pippa Skotnes (ed.), *Miscast: Negotiating the Presence of the Bushmen*, Cape Town: University of Cape Town Press 1996, 41–50.

Gordon, Robert J., *The Bushman Myth: The Making of a Namibian Underclass*, Boulder, San Francisco and Oxford: Westview Press, 1992.

Gordon, Robert J., "The Rise of the Bushman Penis: Germans, Genitalia and Genocide", *African Studies* 55 (1), 1998, 27–53.

Gordon, Robert J., "'Captured on Film': Bushmen and the Claptrap of the Performative Primitive", Paul S. Landau and Deborah D. Kaspin (eds.), *Images and Empires: Visuality in Colonial and Postcolonial Africa*, Berkeley, Los Angeles and London: University of California Press 2002, 212–232.

Gordon, Robert J., "Gathering the Hunters: Bushmen in German (Colonial) Anthropology", Matti Bunzl and Glenn Penny (eds.), *Worldly Provincialism: German Anthropology in the Age of Empire*, Ann Arbor: University of Michigan Press 2003, 261–282.

Gordon, Robert J., "Hiding in Full View: The 'Forgotten' Bushman Genocides of Namibia", *Genocide Studies and Prevention: An International Journal* 4 (1), 2009, n.p.

Grimme, Gesa, "Annäherung an ein 'Schwieriges Erbe': Provenienzforschung im Lindenmuseum Stuttgart", Larissa Förster, Iris Edenheiser, Sarah Fündt and Heike Hartmann (eds.), *Provenienzforschung zu ethnografischen Sammlungen der Kolonialzeit: Positionen in der aktuellen Debatte*, electronic publication for the conference *Provenienzforschung zu ethnografischen Sammlungen der Kolonialzeit*, Munich, 7/8 April 2017, 157–171.

Grimme, Gesa, "Provenienzforschung im Projekt 'Schwieriges Erbe': Zum Umgang mit kolonialzeitlichen Objekten in ethnologischen Museen", unpublished Final Report, Stuttgart: Lindenmuseum, 2018.

Grosfoguel, Ramón, *Colonial Subjects: Puerto Ricans in a Global Perspective*, Berkeley: University of California Press, 2003.

Grosfoguel, Ramón, "The Epistemic Decolonial Turn", *Cultural Studies* 21 (2), 2007, 211–223.

Gschwendtner, Andrea, *Als Anthropologe im Kriegsgefangenenlager: Rudolf Pöchs Filmaufnahmen im Jahre 1915*, accompanying publication to the scientific film P 2208 of the ÖWF, Vienna, 1991.

Gschwendtner, Andrea, "Frühe Wurzeln des Rassismus und Ideologie in der Anthropologie der Jahrhundertwende, am Beispiel des wissenschaftlichen Werkes des Anthropologen und Ethnographen Rudolf Pöch", Claudia Lepp and Barbara Danckwortt (eds.), *Von Grenzen und Ausgrenzung: Interdisziplinäre Beiträge zu den Themen Migration, Minderheiten und Fremdenfeindlichkeit*, Marburg: Schüren 1997, 136–158.

Guenther, Mathias, "From 'Lords of the Desert' to 'Rubbish People': The Colonial and Contemporary State of the Nharo of Botswana", Pippa Skotnes (ed.), *Miscast: Negotiating the Presence of the Bushmen*, Cape Town: University of Cape Town Press 1996, 225–238.

Guenther, Mathias, "'Lords of the Desert Land': Politics and Resistance of the Ghanzi Basarwa of the 19th Century", *Botswana Notes and Records* 29, 1997, 122–141.

Guenther, Mathias, *et al.*, *The Bushmen of Southern Africa: A Foraging Society in Transition*, Cape Town: David Philip, 2000.

Guha, Ranajit, "Chandra's Death", Ranajit Guha (ed.), *Subaltern Studies 5: Writings on South Asian History*, Delhi and Oxford: Oxford University Press 1987, 135–165.

Hallward, Peter: Absolutely Postcolonial: Writing Between the Singular and the Specific, Manchester and New York: Manchester University Press, 2001.

Hamilton, Carolyn, "Backstory, Biography, and the Life of the James Stuart Archive." *History in Africa* 38, 2011, 319–341.

Hamilton, Carolyn, "Forged and Continually Refashioned in the Crucibles of Ongoing Social and Political Life: Archives and Custodial Practices as Subjects of Inquiry", *South African Historical Journal*, 65 (1), 2013, 1–22.

Hamilton, Carolyn, *et al.* (eds.), *Refiguring the Archive*, Cape Town: David Philip, 2002.

Hamilton, Carolyn, and Nessa Leibhammer, "Introduction"', Carolyn Hamilton and Nessa Leibhammer (eds.), *Tribing and Untribing the Archive, Vol. 1*, Pietermaritzburg: University of KZN Press 2015, 13–48.

Harrison, Rodney, "Reassembling the Collection: Ethnographic Museums and Indigenous Agency", Sarah Byrne, Anne Clarke and Rodney Harrison (eds.), *Reassembling the Collection: Ethnographic Museums and Indigenous Agency*, Santa Fe: School for Advanced Research Press 2014, 3-38.

Henrichsen, Dag, *Hans Schinz: Bruchstücke: Forschungsreisen in Deutsch-Südwestafrika*, Basel: Basler Afrika Bibliographien, 2012.

Hiddleston, Jane, "Spivak's 'Echo': Theorizing Otherness and the Space of Response", *Textual Practice* 21 (4), 2007, 623–640.

Hilden, Irene, "Who sang this song? An acoustic testimony between self-empowerment and object status", Anna-Maria Brandstetter and Vera Hierholzer (eds.), *Nicht nur Raubkunst! Sensible Dinge in Museen und universitären Sammlungen*, Mainz: Mainz University Press, 2018, 177–194.

Hirschberg, Walter, *Völkerkundliche Ergebnisse der südafrikanischen Reisen Rudolf Pöchs in den Jahren 1907 bis 1909*, Vienna: Verlag der Anthropologischen Gesellschaft, 1936.

Hoffmann, Anette, "Finding Words (of Anger)", Anette Hoffmann (ed.), *What We See: Reconsidering an Anthropometrical Collection from Southern Africa: Images, Voices and Versioning*, Basel: Basler Afrika Bibliographien 2009, 114–144.

Hoffmann, Anette, "Widerspenstige Stimmen/Unruly Voices", Anette Hoffmann (ed.), *What We See: Reconsidering an Anthropometrical Collection from Southern Africa: Images, Voices and Versioning*, Basel: Basler Afrika Bibliographien 2009, 22–57.

Hoffmann, Anette, "Glaubwürdige Inszenierungen: Die Produktion von Abformungen in der Polizeistation von Keetmanshoop im August 1931", Margit Berner, Anete Hoffmann and Britta Lange, *Sensible Sammlungen: Aus dem anthropologischen Depot*, Hamburg: Philo Fine Arts 2011, 61–88.

Hoffmann, Anette, "'Oh meine Schwester, mein Rücken brennt sehr, und ich bin machtlos!' Voice Over I, Haneb", Margit Berner, Anete Hoffmann and Britta Lange, *Sensible Sammlungen: Aus dem anthropologischen Depot*, Hamburg: Philo Fine Arts 2011, 129–146.

Hoffmann, Anette, "'Wie ein Hund in einem Fangeisen schreien': *Voice Over* II, Kanaje", Margit Berner, Anette Hoffmann and Britta Lange, *Sensible Sammlungen: Aus dem anthropologischen Depot*, Hamburg: Philo Fine Arts 2011, 169–184.

Hoffmann, Anette, "Verbale Riposte: Wilfred Tjiuezas Performances von omitandu als Entgegnungen zum Rassenmodell Hans Lichteneckers", Iris Dressler and Hans D. Christ (eds.), *Acts of Voicing*, Stuttgart: Hatje Cantz 2014, 141–153.

Hoffmann, Anette, "Listening to Sound Archives: Introduction to Edited Section", *Social Dynamics* 41 (1), 2015: *Special Section Listening to Sound Archives*, 73–83.

Hoffmann, Anette, "Of Storying and Storing: 'Reading' Lichtenecker's Voice Recordings", Jeremy Silvester (ed.), *Re-Viewing Resistance in Namibian History*, Windhoek: UNAM Press, 2015, 89–104.

Hoffmann, Anette, "Echoes of the Great War: The Recording of African Prisoners in the First World War", Leon Wainwright (ed.), *Disturbing Pasts: Memories, Controversies and Creativity*, Manchester: Manchester University Press 2018, 11–35.

Hoffmann, Anette, "Kolonialität", Daniel Morat and Hansjakob Ziemer (eds.), *Handbuch Sound: Geschichte - Begriffe - Ansätze*, Stuttgart: Metzler 2018, 387–390.

Hoffmann, Anette, "'Achtung Aufnahme!' Akustische Spuren kolonialer Wissensproduktion", Iris Edenheiser and Larissa Förster (eds.), *Museumsethnologie: Eine Einführung: Theorien - Debatten - Praktiken*, Berlin: Dietrich Reimer Verlag, 2019, 204–205.

Hoffmann, Anette, *Kolonialgeschichte hören: Das Echo gewaltsamer Wissensproduction in historischen Tondokumenten aus dem südlichen Afrika*, Vienna: Mandelbaum, 2020.

Hoffmann, Anette, "War and Grammar: Acoustic Recordings with African Prisoners of the First World War (1915—18)", Ana Deumert, Anne Storch and Nick Shepherd (eds.), *Colonial and Decolonial Linguistics: Knowledges and Epistemes*, London: Oxford University Press, 2020.

Hoffmann, Anette, "Close Listening: Approaches to Research on Colonial Sound Archives", Marcel Cobussen and Michael Bull (eds.), *The Bloomsbury Handbook of Sonic Methodologies*, New York and London: Bloomsbury, 2021, 529–539.

Hoffmann, Anette, "Skandalträchtig Drauflosreden: Vorschläge zur Entsachlichung des Sprechens von der Erbeutung von Körpern, Objekten, und von Praktiken der kolonialen Linguistik, in vier Stücken", *The Mouth: Critical Studies on Language, Culture and Society* 9, 2021, 11–30.

Hoffmann, Anette, *Knowing by Ear: Listening to voice recordings with African prisoners of war in German Camps (1915–1918)*, Durham: Duke University Press, forthcoming.

Hoffmann, Anette and Phindezwa Mnyaka, "Hearing Voices in the Archive", *Social Dynamics* 41 (1), 2015: *Special Section Listening to Sound Archives*, 101–123.

Hoffmann, Anette, Regina Sarreiter and Britta Lange, *Was Wir Sehen: Bilder, Stimmen, Rauschen: Zur Kritik anthropometrischen Sammelns*, Basel: Basler Afrika Bibliographien 2012.

Institut für Lautforschung an der Universität Berlin (ed.), "Xhosa in Südafrika: Aufgenommen von Prof. Dr. C. Meinhof, bearbeitet von Dr. A. N. Tucker", *Lautbibliothek: Texte zu den Sprachplatten des Institutes für Lautforschung*, edited by D. Westermann 1936.

Ivanov, Paola and Kristin Weber-Sinn, "Shared Research: Zur Notwendigkeit einer kooperativen Provenienzforschung am Beispiel der Tansania-Projekte am Ethnologischen Museum Berlin", *Provenienzforschung zu ethnografischen Sammlungen der Kolonialzeit: Positionen in der aktuellen Debatte*, electronic publication for the conference *Provenienzforschung zu ethnografischen Sammlungen der Kolonialzeit*, Munich, 7/8 April 2017, 143–157.

Kalibani, Méhéza, "Kolonialer Tinnitus: Das belastende Geräusch des Kolonialismus." *Geschichte in Wissenschaft und Unterrricht* 9/10, 2021, 540–553.

Kaufmann, Hans, "Die Aunin: Ein Beitrag zur Buschmannforschung", *Mitteilungen aus den Deutschen Schutzgebieten* 23, 1910, 135–160.

Kolesch, Doris and Sybille Krämer (eds.), *Stimme*, Frankfurt am Main: Suhrkamp, 2006.

Lalu, Premesh, "Sara's Suicide: History and the Representational Limit", *Kronos* 26, 2000, 89–101.

Lalu, Premesh, *The Deaths of Hintsa: Postapartheid South Africa and the Shape of Recurring Pasts*, Cape Town: HSRC Press, 2009.

Landau, Paul S., "With Camera and Gun in Southern Africa: Inventing the Image of the Bushman c. 1880 to 1935", Pippa Skotnes (ed.), *Miscast:*

Negotiating the Presence of the Bushmen, Cape Town: University of Cape Town Press 1996, 129–143.

Landau, Paul S., *Popular Politics in the History of South Africa 1400–1948,* Cambridge and New York: Cambridge University Press, 2010.

Lange, Britta, "'Denken sie selbst über die Sache nach': Tonaufnahmen in deutschen Gefangenenlagern des Ersten Weltkriegs", Margit Berner, Anette Hoffmann and Britta Lange, *Sensible Sammlungen: Aus dem anthropologsischen Depot,* Hamburg: Philo Fine Arts 2011, 89–128.

Lange, Britta, "South Asian Soldiers and German Academics: Anthropological, Linguistic and Musicological Field Studies in Prison Camps", Ravi Ahuja, Heike Liebau and Franziska Roy (eds.), *'When the War Began, We Heard of Several Kings': South Asian Prisoners in World War I Germany,* Delhi: Social Science Press 2011, 149–186.

Lange, Britta, *Die Wiener Forschungen an Kriegsgefangenen 1915–1918: Anthropologische und ethnographische Verfahren im Lager,* Vienna: OAW Verlag, 2013.

Lange, Britta, "Poste Restante, and Messages in Bottles: Sound Recordings of Indian Prisoners in the First World War", *Social Dynamics* 41 (1), 2015: *Special Section Listening to Sound Archives,* 84–100.

Lange, Britta, "Archiv", Daniel Morat and Hansjakob Ziemer (eds.), *Handbuch Sound: Geschichte - Begriffe - Ansätze,* Stuttgart: Metzler 2018, 236–240.

Lange, Britta, *Gefangene Stimmen: Tonaufnahmnen von Kriegsgefangenen aus dem Lautarchiv, 1915-1918,* Berlin: Kadmos Verlag, 2020.

Lautabteilung der Preußischen Staatsbibliothek, "Mandara, aufgezeichnet von Carl Meinhof, bearbeitet von August Klingenheben", *Phonetische Platten und Umschriften* No. 48, 1929.

Lechleitner, Gerda, "Pöch, Rudolf", Österreichisches Musiklexikon online, https://www.musiklexikon.ac.at/ml/musik_P/Poech_Rudolf. xml, last modified 2001.

Le Guin, Ursula K, *The Carrier Bag Theory of Fiction,* introduced by Donna Haraway, New Castle upon Tyne: Ignota, 2019.

Lichtenstein, Hinrich, *Reisen im südlichen Africa in den Jahren 1803, 1804, 1805 und 1806, Zweiter Theil,* Berlin: 1812.

Luschan, Felix von, "Bericht über eine Reise in Südafrika", *Zeitschrift für Ethnologie* 38 (6), 1906, 863–95.

Luschan, Felix von, *Anleitung zu wissenschaftlichen Beobachtungen auf dem Gebiet der Anthropologie, Ethnographie und Urgeschichte*, Berlin 1910.

Luschan, Felix von, "Pygmäen und Buschmänner", *Zeitschrift für Ethnologie* 46 (4), 1914, 154–176.

Matiasek, Katarina, "A Mutual Space? Stereo Photography on Viennese Anthropological Expeditions (1905–1945)", Marianne Kleum and Ulrike Spring (eds.), *Expeditions as Experiments: Practising Observation and Documentation*, London: Palgrave Macmillan, 2016 187–212.

Mbembe, Achille, *Kritik der schwarzen Vernunft*, Berlin: Suhrkamp, 2014.

Mokibelo, Eureka Baneka, "Why We Drop Out of School: Voices of San School Drop Outs in Botswana", *Australian Journal of Indigenous Education*, 43 (2), 2014, 185–194.

Moran, Shane, *Representing Bushmen: South Africa and the Origin of Language*, Rochester, NY: University of Rochester Press, 2009.

Morris, Rosalind C., "Introduction", Rosalind Morris (ed.), *Can the Subaltern Speak? Reflections on the History of an Idea*, New York: Columbia University Press 2010, 1–20.

Müller, Franz F., *Kolonien unter der Peitsche*, Berlin: Rütten and Loening, 1962.

Muschalek, Marie, *Violence as Usual: Policing and the Colonial State in German Southwest Africa*, Ithaka and London: Cornell University Press, 2019.

Oksiloff, Assenka, *Picturing the Primitive: Visual Culture, Ethnography and Early German Cinema*, New York: Palgrave MacMillan, 2001.

Pacher, Helga Maria, *Anthropologische Untersuchungen an den Skeletten der Rudolf Pöch'schen Buschmannsammlung, 1. Heft: Herkunft des Sammlungsgutes, Maßbefunde und Lichtbilder der Schädel*, Österreichische Akademie der Wissenschaften, Rudolf Pöchs Nachlass, Serie A: Physische Anthropologie, XII, Band, Graz, Vienna and Cologne: Böhlau, 1962.

Pandey, Gyanendra, "Voices from the Edge: The Struggle to Write Subaltern Histories" (2000), Vinayak Chaturvedi (ed.), *Mapping Subaltern Studies and the Postcolonial*, London: Verso, 2012, 281–299.

. Passarge, Siegfried, *Die Kalahari: Versuch einer physisch-geographischen Darstellung der Sandfelder des südafrikanischen Beckens*, Berlin: Dietrich Reimer Verlag, 1904.

Passarge, Siegfried, *Die Buschmänner der Kalahari*, Berlin: Dietrich Reiner Verlag, 1907.

Peeren, Esther, *Intersubjectivities and Popular Culture: Bakhtin and Beyond*, Stanford: Stanford University Press, 2008.

Peeren, Esther, "Seeing more (Hi)Stories: Versioning as Resignificatory Practice in the *What We See* Exhibttion and the Work of Sanell Aggenbach and Mustafa Maluka", Anette Hoffmann (ed.), *What We See: Reconsidering an Anthropometrical Collection from Southern Africa, Images, Voices and Versioning*, Basel: Basler Afrika Bibliographien 2009, 84–104.

Penn, Nigel, "'Fated to Perish': The Destruction of the Cape San", Pippa Skotnes (ed.), *Miscast: Negotiating the Presence of the Bushmen*, Cape Town: University of Cape Town Press 1996, 81–92.

Penn, Nigel, *The Forgotten Frontier: Colonists and Khoisan on the Cape's Northern Frontier in the 18th Century*. Athens and Cape Town: Ohio University Press and Double Storey Books, 2005.

Phadi, Mosa, and Nomancotsho Pacade, "The Native Informant Speaks Back to the Offer of Friendship in White Academia", Shannon Walsh & Jon Soske (eds.), *Ties that Bind: Race and the Politics of Friendship in South Africa*, Johannesburg: Wits University Press 2016, 288–307.

Plankensteiner, Barbara, "'Auch hier gilt die Regel, Buschmanngut und Fremdgut auseinanderzuhalten': Rudolf Pöchs Südafrika-Sammlung und ihre wissenschaftliche Bearbeitung durch Walter Hirschberg", *Archiv für Völkerkunde* 59-60, 2009, 95–107.

Pöch, Rudolf, unpublished notebooks, numbers 1, 2, 7, 8, 9, 10, 11, 12, 13, 14, Naturhistorisches Museum, Vienna, 1907–1909.

Pöch, Rudolf, "Berichte an die Akademie", *Anzeiger der Akademie der Wissenschaften*, XLV. Jahrgang, 1908.

Pöch, Rudolf, "Berichte an die Akademie", *Anzeiger der Akademie der Wissenschaften*, XLVI. Jahrgang, 1909.

Pöch, Rudolf, "Meine beiden Kalahari Reisen 1908 und 1909", *Zeitschrift für Erdkunde zu Berlin*, 1910, 24-35.

Pöch, Rudolf, "Reisen im Inneren Südafrikas zum Studium der Buschmänner in den Jahren 1907 bis 1909", meeting of 19 February 1910, *Zeitschrift für Ethnologie* 42 (2), 1910, 57–361.

Pöch, Rudolf, "Die Stellung der Buschmannrasse unter den übrigen Menschenrassen", *Korrespondenzblatt der Deutschen Gesellschaft für Anthropologie, Ethnologie und Urgeschichte* 42, 1911, 8–12.

Pöch, Rudolf, "Technik und Wert des Sammelns phonographischer Sprachproben auf Expeditionen", *45th Mitteilungen der Phonogram-*

marchivs-Kommission der kaiserlichen Akademie der Wissenschaften in Wien, 1917, 1–13.

Prakash, Gyan, "Subaltern Studies as Postcolonial Criticism", *American Historical Review* 99 (5), 1994, 1475–1490.

Prakash, Gyan, "The Impossibility of Subaltern History", *Nepantla* 1 (2), 2000, 287–294.

Pratt, Mary Louise, *Imperial Eyes: Travel Writing and Transculturation*, London and New York: Routledge 1992.

Quijano, Aníbal, "The Coloniality of Power, Eurocentrism, and Latin America", *Nepantla* 1 (3), 2000, 533–580.

Quijano, Aníbal, "Coloniality and Modernity/Rationality", *Cultural Studies* 21 (2-3), 2007, 168–178.

Rancière, Jacques, *Das Unvernehmen*, Frankfurt am Main: Suhrkamp, 1995.

Rassool, Ciraj, "Restoring the Skeletons of Empire: Return, Reburial and Rehumanisation", *Journal of Southern African Studies* 41 (3), 2015, 653–670.

Rassool, Ciraj, and Martin Legassick, *Skeletons in the Cupboard: South African Museums and the Trade in Human Remains 1907–1917*, Cape Town and Kimberley: The South African Museum 2000.

Rensing, Julia, Lorena Rizzo and Wanda Rutishauser (eds.), *Sites of Contestation: Encounters with the Ernst and Ruth Dammann Collection in the Archives of the Basler Afrika Bibliographien*, Basel: Basler Afrika Bibliographien, 2021.

Sacken, Katharina, "Ungern vor Fremden gesungen: Koloniale Phonographie um 1900", *Phonorama: Eine Kulturgeschichte der Stimme als Medium*, Berlin: Matthes & Seitz 2004, 118–131.

Sarr, Felwine and Bénédicte Savoy, *Zurückgeben: Über die Restitution Afrikanischer Kulturgüter*, Berlin: Matthes and Seitz, 2019.

Sarreiter, Regina, "Activate Facts! Von sprechenden Tatsachen", Martina Griesser *et al.* (eds.), *Gegen den Stand der Dinge: Objekte in Museen und Ausstellungen*, Berlin: De Gruyter 2016, 115–128.

Sauer, Walther, "Die Geschichte von Klaas und Trooi Pienaar", *INDABA* 74 (12), 2012, 3–8.

Schasiepen, Sophie, *Schreiben über Dr Rudolf Pöch's 'Forschungsreisen': Postkoloniale Kritiken und die österreichische Rezeption einen k.u.k. Anthropologen, Eine kritische Diskursanalyse*, unpublished diploma thesis, Academy of Fine Arts Vienna, 2013.

Schasiepen, Sophie, "Die 'Lehrmittelsammlungen' von Dr. Rudolf Pöch an der Universität Wien: Anthropologie, Forensik und Provenienz", *Journal of Cultural Studies* 1, 2019, 15–28.

Schasiepen, Sophie, *Southern African Human Remains as Property: Physical Anthropology and the Production of Racial Capital in Austria*, Ph.D. thesis, Department of History, University of the Western Cape, South Africa, 2021.

Schramm, Katharina, "Neue Technologien - Alte Kategorien? Die Problematisierung von Rasse an der Schnittstelle von Wissenschaft und Politik", *Zeitschrift für Ethnologie* 139 (5), 2014, 233–252.

Schüller, Dietrich (ed.), *Rudolf Pöch's Kalahari Recordings (1908): Sound Documents from the Phonogrammarchiv of the Austrian Academy of Sciences: The Complete Historical Collections 1899–1950, Series 7*, Vienna: OAW, 2003.

Schultze, Leonhard, *Aus Namaland und Kalahari: Bericht an die Kgl. Preuss, Akademie der Wissenschaften über eine Forschungsreise im westlichen u. zentralen Südafrika, ausgeführt in den Jahren 1903–1905*, Jena: Fischer, 1907.

Scott, Joan W., "Fantasy Echo: History and the Construction of Identity", *Critical Inquiry* 27 (2), 2001, 284–304.

Seiner, Franz, "Die Bastard Buschleute der Nord-Kalahari", *Mitteilungen aus den deutschen Schutzgebieten* 26 (3), 1913, 227–316.

Seiner, Franz, and Peter Staudinger, "Observations and Measurements on Bushmen", *Journal of Ethnology* 44 (2), 1912, 275–288.

Shepherd, Nick, *The Mirror in the Ground: Archaeology, Photography and the Making of a Disciplinary Archive*, Jeppestown: Jonathan Ball, 2015.

Simon, Artur (ed.), *Das Berliner Phonogramm-Archiv 1900-2000: Sammlungen der traditionellen Musik der Welt*, Berlin: Verlag für Wissenschaft und Bildung, 2000.

Skotnes, Pippa (ed.), *Claim to the Country: The Archive of Lucy Lloyd and Wilhelm Bleek*, Johannesburg: Jacana Publishers, 2007.

Smith, Linda Tuhiwai, *Decolonizing Methodologies: Research and Indigenous People*, London: Zed Books, 1999.

Sonderegger, Ruth, "What One Does (Not) Hear: Approaching Canned Voices Through Rancière", Anette Hoffmann (ed.): *What We See: Reconsidering an Anthropometrical Collection: Images, Voices and Versioning*, Basel: Basler Afrika Bibliographien, 2009, 58–84.

Sonderegger, Ruth, *Vom Leben der Kritik: Kritische Praktiken und die Notwendigkeit ihrer geopolitischen Situierung*, Wien: Zaglossus, 2019.

Spivak, Gayatri C., "The Rani of Simur: An Essay in Reading the Archives", *History and Theory* 24 (3), 1985, 247–272.

Spivak, Gayatri C., "Can the Subaltern Speak?", C. Nelson and L. Grossberg (eds.), *Marxism and the Interpretation of Cultures*, Basingstoke: Macmillan 1988, 271–233.

Spivak, Gayatri C., "Echo", *New Literary Review: Culture and Everyday Life* 24 (1), 1993, 17-43.

Spivak, Gayatri C., *A Critique of Postcolonial Reason: Toward a History of the Vanishing Present*, Cambridge, Massachusetts, and London: Harvard University Press, 1999.

Spivak, Gayatri C., "In Response: Looking Back, Looking Forward", Rosalind C. Morris (ed.), *Can the Subaltern Speak? Reflections on the History of an Idea*, New York: Columbia University Press 2010, 227–236.

Stangl, Burkhardt, *Ethnologie im Ohr: Die Wirkungsgeschichte des Phonographen*, Vienna: WUV Verlag, 2000.

Steedman, Carolyn, "Enforced Narratives: Stories of Another Self", Tess Cosslett, Celia Lury and Penny Summerfield (eds.), *Feminism and Autobiography: Texts, Theories, Methods*, London: Routledge 2000, 25–29.

Sterne, Jonathan, *The Audible Past: Cultural Origins of Sound Reproduction*, Durham: Duke University Press 2003.

Stoecker, Holger, "Human Remains as Historical Sources for Namibian-German History: Results and Experiences from an Interdisciplinary Research Project", Geert Castryck, Silke Strickrodt and Katja Werthmann (eds.), *Sources and Methods for African History and Culture: Essays in Honor of Adam Jones*, Leipzig: Leipziger Universitätsverlag 2016, 469–492.

Stoecker, Holger, Thomas Schnalke and Andreas Winkelmann (eds.), *Sammeln, Erforschen, Zurückgeben? Menschliche Gebeine aus der Kolonialzeit in akademischen und musealen Sammlungen*, Berlin: Ch. Links Verlag, 2013.

Stoecker, Holger, and Vilho Shigwedha, "Human Remains in German Collections", *Human Remains and Violence* 4 (2), 2018, n.p.

Stoever, Jennifer, *The Sonic Color Line: Race and the Cultural Politics of Listening*, New York: New York University Press, 2016.

Stoler, Ann Laura, *Along the Archival Grain: Epistemic Anxieties and Colonial Common Sense*, Princeton and London: Princeton University Press, 2009.

Stoler, Ann Laura, "Colonial Aphasia: Race and Disabled History in France", *Public Culture* 23 (1), 2011, 121–156.

Stoler, Ann Laura, *Duress: Imperial Durabilities in Our Times*, Durham and London: Duke University Press, 2016.

Szilvásy, Johann, Paul Spindler and Herbert Kritschler, "Rudolf Pöch: Arzt, Anthropologe und Ethnograph", *Annalen des Naturhistorischen Museums in Wien* 83, 1980, 743–762.

Taussig, Michael, *Mimesis and Alterity: A Particular History of the Senses*, New York and London: Routledge, 1993.

Titus, Barbara and meLê Yamomo, "The Persistent Refrain of the Colonial Archival Logic/Colonial Entanglements and Sonic Transgressions: Sounding out the Jaap Kunst Collection", *World of Music* 10 (1) 2021, 39–72.

Trouillot, Michel-Rolph, *Silencing the Past: Power and the Production of History*, Boston: Beacon Press, 1995.

Vail, Leroy and Landeg White, *Power and the Praise Poem: Southern African Voices in History*, London: James Currey, 1991.

Weidmann, Amanda, "Voice", David Novak and Matt Sakakeeny (eds.), *Keywords in Sound*, Durham and London: Duke University Press, 2015, 232–245.

Weinstein, Valerie, "Archiving the Ephemeral: Dance in Ethnographic Films from the Hamburg South Seas Expedition 1908–1910", *Seminar* 46 (3), 2010, 223–239.

Weintroub, Jill, *Dorothea Bleek: A Life of Scholarship, A Biography*, Johannesburg: Wits University Press, 2016.

Weninger, Josef, *Eine morphologisch-anthropologische Studie: Durchgeführt an 100 westafrikanischen Negern, als Beitrag zur Anthropologie von Afrika*, Vienna: Verlag der Anthropologischen Gesellschaft 1926.

Wernsing, Susanne, Christian Geulen and Klaus Vogel, *Rassismus: Die Erfindung von Menschenrassen; Begleitband für die gleichnamige Ausstellung im Deutschen Hygiene-Museum Dresden*, Göttingen: Wallstein Verlag, 2018.

Wessels, Michael, *Bushman Letters: Interpreting |Xam Letters*, Johannesburg: Wits University Press, 2010.

White, Luise, *Speaking with Vampires: Rumor and History in Colonial Africa*, Berkeley and Los Angeles: University of California Press, 2000.

Wiesner, Polly, "Hunting, Healing, and Hxaro Exchange: A Long-Term Perspective on !Kung (Ju/'hoansi) Large-Game Hunting", *Evolution and Human Behavior* 23, 2002, 407–436.

Witz, Leslie and Ciraj Rassool, "Making Histories", *Kronos* 34, 2008, 6–15.

Zastrow, Berengar von, "Über die Buschleute", *Zeitschrift für Ethnologie* 46 (1), 1914, 1–7.

Ziegler, Susanne, *Die Wachszylinder des Berliner Phonogramm-Archivs*, Berlin: Veröffentlichungen des Ethnologischen Museums Berlin, 2006.

Ziegler, Susanne, "Felix von Luschan als Walzensammler und Förderer des Berliner Phonogramm-Archivs", Peter Ruggendorfer and Hubert D. Szemethy (eds.), *Felix von Luschan (1854–1924): Leben und Wirken eines Universalgelehrten*, Vienna: Böhlau 2009, 113–141.

Zimmer, Niklas, "Percival Kirby's Wax Cylinders: Elegy On Archiving a Deaf Spot", *Social Dynamics* 41 (1), 2015: *Special Section Listening to Sound Archives*, 101–123.

Zimmermann, Andrew, "Adventures in the Skin Trade: German Anthropology and Colonial Corporeality", Glenn Penny and Matti Bunzl (eds.), *Worldly Provincialism: German Anthropology in the Age of Empire*, Ann Arbor: The University of Michigan Press 2003, 156–178.

Printed in the United States
by Baker & Taylor Publisher Services